P9-CDM-082

MUZZLELOADING

BY TOBY BRIDGES

CREATIVE
PUBLISHING
international

MINNETONKA, MINNESOTA

www.howtobookstore.com

TOBY BRIDGES has hunted throughout North America with all types of black powder guns, but he prefers a modern, in-line muzzleloading rifle. He began using muzzleloaders in his home state of Illinois in the mid-1960s. An outdoor writer for more than 30 years, Toby has authored over 1,000 muzzleloading articles.

President/CEO: David D. Murphy
Vice President/Editorial: Patricia K. Jacobsen
Vice President/Retail Sales & Marketing: Richard M. Miller

MUZZLELOADING
By Toby Bridges

Executive Editor, Outdoor Products Group: Don Oster
Editorial Director: David R. Maas
Managing Editor: Jill Anderson
Editor: Steven Hauge
Creative Director: Bradley Springer
Senior Art Director: David Schelitzche
Art Director: Joe Fahey
Photo Researcher: Angela Hartwell
Studio Manager: Marcia Chambers
Studio Services Coordinator: Carol Osterhus
Principal Photographer: Mark Macemon
Staff Photographers: Mike Hehner, Bill Lindner, Charles Nields, Andrea Rugg
Photo Assistants: Dan Cary, Vance Dovenbarger, Frederick Stroebel, Keith Zilinski
Director, Production Services: Kim Gerber
Production Staff: Nicole Hepokoski, Laura Hokkanen, Helga Thielen
Contributing Photographers: Charles J. Alsheimer, Toby Bridges, Gary Clancy, Bill Kinney, Stephen W. Maas, Paramount Press, Inc., James P. Rowan Photography, Ira Rubin Photography, Leonard Rue Enterprises, Inc.
Contributing Manufacturers: Browning/U.S. Repeating Arms; Cabela's, Inc.; Connecticut Valley Arms, Inc. – Bob Hickey, Dave Meredith; Dixie Gun Works, Inc. – Hunter Kirkland, George "Butch" Winter, and the entire staff; The Farrel Group – Kevin Howard; Hodgdon Powder Co., Inc. – Chris Hodgdon; Hoppe's – Penguin Industries, Inc.; Knight Rifles – Michele Bartimus, William "Tony" Knight; Mountain State Muzzleloading Supplies, Inc. – Fred Lambert; Pentax Corporation; Redfield, Inc.; Savage Arms Inc. – Tom Mihalek; Thompson/Center Arms Co., Inc. – Eric E. Brooker; Track of the Wolf, Inc. – David S. Ripplinger, Ethan R. Ripplinger, Jonathan Wheeler; Traditions, Inc. – Jay Brenneman
Contributing Individuals and Agencies: Adam Bridges; Gary Clancy; David A. Ehrig; John Goodwin; International Blackpowder Hunting Association – Debra Bradbury; John and Billy Knight; Frank Maas; National Muzzle Loading Rifle Association – Denise Goodpaster, Terry Trowbridge; North-South Skirmish Association, Inc. – Bruce Miller; Outdoor Media Resources – Rori L. Chandler; Outdoor Writers Association of America – Steve Wagner; Paramount Press, Inc. – Dana Nordlund, Jerry Seymour; Brett Schelitzche; Jeff Simpson; Pat & Tom Wagamon

Printed on American paper by: R. R. Donnelley & Sons Co.
10 9 8 7 6 5 4 3 2 1

Copyright © 2000 by Creative Publishing international, Inc.
5900 Green Oak Drive
Minnetonka, MN 55343
1-800-328-3895
www.howtobookstore.com

Library of Congress Cataloging-in-Publication Data
Bridges, Toby.
    Muzzleloading / by Toby Bridges.
        p. cm. -- (The Complete hunter)
        Originally published: Minnetonka, MN : Cowles Creative Pub., c1997, in series: The Hunting & fishing library. The complete hunter)
    ISBN 0-86573-127-6
    1. Muzzleloader hunting. 2. Muzzle-loading firearms. I. Title. II. Complete hunter (Creative Publishing International)
SK39.2 .B74 2000
799.2'028'3--dc21   00-063856

Contents

Introduction

Muzzleloading. The word alone conjures up visions of buckskin-clad explorers crossing an untamed wilderness. Or, perhaps you are reminded of the Civil War soldier who fought in bloody conflicts that often pitted brother against brother on the battlefield. Muzzleloading firearms originated in Europe shortly before Christopher Columbus set sail for the Americas, and they went on to play an instrumental role in the shaping of our history. For thousands of black powder shooters, muzzleloading serves as a link to these long-past eras.

Although nostalgia was a major factor in why many shooters during the 1960s and 70s turned to muzzleloading, it now plays a much smaller role. Today's black powder shooter is a hunter. More specifically, he is a white-tail deer hunter who has turned to muzzleloading in order to participate in the special "muzzleloader-only" hunts now held in nearly every state.

Today's hunter is less concerned about the authentic styling of the muzzleloader he carries into the woods. More important is how the muzzleloader performs. And the modern-day hunter is making new demands on muzzleloader performance, striving for 100-yard accuracy that a few years ago could only be obtained with a quality centerfire rifle. There is now a new breed of muzzleloading hunting rifle that is fully capable of shooting 1½-inch groups at that distance.

Combine the sudden popularity of hunting deer and other big game with a muzzleloading rifle featuring recent advances in muzzleloader design, and you have the fastest growing and changing of today's shooting and hunting sports. A long list of states currently issue more than 100,000 muzzleloading permits each fall.

This book covers the fascinating sport of muzzleloading, from the development of the earliest-known firearms to the modernistic, scope-sighted muzzleloaders of today. In these pages, you will find all the information needed to take one of today's muzzleloaders right from the box and begin shooting the gun successfully – regardless of whether it is a reproduction of a traditionally styled gun from the past or one of the popular in-line rifles. You'll also learn about cutting-edge firearm advancements in the special section, "Muzzleloading into the 21st Century."

The full enjoyment of muzzleloading begins with the satisfaction that comes from properly selecting the rifle, pistol, shotgun or musket that best fits your needs. Understanding the history of muzzleloader development and how each of the different ignition systems function is the first step toward making the right choice.

The hunter looking for optimum performance from a muzzleloader should first determine which type of projectile will be used. It takes an entirely different rifle to get the best accuracy from a patched round ball, a bore-sized conical bullet, or a saboted pistol bullet. Another important consideration is the caliber of any rifle to be used on game. This book will help you choose the best combination for hunting every popular species.

Traditional or modern, muzzleloading offers today's shooter a challenge. This book details the "how-to" of loading and maintenance, the accessories that make muzzleloading easier and more enjoyable, tips and techniques for better accuracy and how to develop effective hunting loads. *Muzzleloading* is sure to make your black powder shooting and hunting not only more enjoyable, but more productive as well.

Muzzleloading, Past & Present

The History of Muzzleloaders

Whenever you pick up a muzzleloader, you are literally holding 700 years of European and American history in your hands. How muzzleloaders came to be is the fascinating story of human ingenuity and problem solving bolstered by scientific discoveries and, quite often, plain pure luck. From the beginning of development in the 1300s down to the present day, inventors of black powder smoothbore and rifled muzzleloaders have asked and answered the same fundamental question: "How can I make the gun better?"

Designs for portable muzzleloaders progressed from heavy iron hand cannons, to lightweight longarms to, finally, pistols requiring only the hand, thumb and index finger. These designs influenced the evolution of seven *locks,* or ignition systems, each one either better than its predecessor or having a feature that contributed to its successor. Improvements in overall gun designs and lock systems increased muzzleloader accuracy as the centuries passed.

To recapture the history of the muzzleloader, we'll begin at the explosive beginning: the creation of black powder. We'll take a brief look at how black powder became gunpowder, cannons became hand-held, and hand cannons eventually became single-shot smoothbore muzzleloading muskets.

Triumphant Return to Fort Duquesne, by Robert Griffing, depicts a victorious procession during the French and Indian War (1754-63). The Indians, who were allies of the French against the British, return triumphantly to the French fort (modern Pittsburgh, PA) after ambushing the British. The day's spoils include British Brown Bess muskets, red coats, sabers and canteens.

Triumphant Return to Fort Duquesne, by Robert Griffing, is a limited edition print published by Paramount Press, Inc.

8

Black Powder and Cannons

In the year 1242, English friar-philosopher Roger Bacon wrote down the short recipe for Chinese snow that he had been reading about in Latin manuscripts. It was a low-explosive substance created in China and used in Rome for fireworks during the previous 200 years. Renamed "black powder," it was destined to alter forever the nature of warfare and hunting. One of the true world-changers, black powder still hasn't changed its composition – just how it's made and the possible proportions of the ingredients.

Mix together in proportioned amounts three common ingredients – saltpeter, ground charcoal and sulfur – and you'll have a slow-burning explosive that can be used to set off an even larger charge of the same mixture. Placed inside a wrought-iron tube or barrel, black powder could (and did) fire a 550-pound stone ball 2800 yards.

What is known about early cannons comes from medieval manuscripts of the period just after Bacon wrote down and shared the formula for what was by then called gunpowder. The first illustration of a cannon was drawn in 1326; the English used cannons in the 1346 battle of Crécy during the Hundred Years' War; the Turks followed suit when they captured Constantinople in 1453.

Stationary-mounted in large wooden trough carriages, cannons were wrought-metal muzzleloaders with stone or iron ball projectiles. The iron, bronze or brass barrel was molded up of strips and hoops (modeled on beer casks) reaching very large calibers. The breech end was closed except for a touchhole (vent)

opening to the barrel's chamber. Because the primary use of cannons in the 1300s was to batter down walls in static sieges to make way for ensuing hand-to-hand combat, they only needed to be aligned directly at the target for days on end of repeated firing. Wheels were added to carriages in the 1400s mainly for long-distance transport.

The loading and firing of early cannons was done strictly by hand, by a team of cannoneers. First, the powder (bagged in linen or loose) and shot were separately lifted and pushed through the muzzle, down the barrel, with a wooden rammer, while another man covered the vent with his thumb, protected by a leather thumbstall. Next, the vent was exposed and

primed with a measure of finer-grained gunpowder, which was then touched off by a match. A match was a long wick or twisted cord especially treated to burn slowly and steadily when lit at the end, similar to monks' candlelamp tapers. The match obtained its source of fire from a coal- or wood-burning metal pan called a *frypanne*. Once the primer ignited, the flash detonated the main charge, and the explosion of its gases propelled the shot toward its target.

During the earliest years of the cannon's appearance, several unknown individuals living somewhere in Europe conceptualized and began working with the notion that all the principles of the cannon could be miniaturized into a portable, hand-held firearm.

Hand Cannons

Although records concerning the exact origin of the hand cannon are nonexistent, scattered surviving art and documentary evidence indicates that hand-held muzzleloaders were becoming common in Europe by 1375. English King Edward II made use of them in his 1327 invasion of Scotland, just 1 year after the first illustration of a cannon appeared. Paolo del Maestro Neri's paintings on St. Leonardo's monastery walls in Lacetto, Germany, are dated to 1340–43. They clearly depict soldiers carrying and firing small handgun tubes about 3 feet long. Written documentation also verifies the use of hand-held firearms at Perugia, Italy, in 1364. The single-shot, muzzleloading, smoothbore longarm began with the crude hand cannon and became the basic firearm all over the world for the next 400 years.

The first hand cannons of the late fourteenth and early fifteenth centuries were heavy wrought-iron pipes in varying dimensions exhibiting regional differences in design and names. Typically, an iron hook projecting downward was fastened to the front end just behind the muzzle. This was positioned over a portable rest or tripod support to absorb the recoil. Projectiles were round stone or iron balls. Wooden stocks fitted to the barrel aided in aiming the hand cannon. Steps such as loading powder and shot, igniting the primer through a touchhole and swabbing out the barrel between shots were all done in the same manner as for the large cannons. These early muzzleloaders were developed for military use and, as yet, had no mechanics.

Heavy, undependable and inaccurate, hand cannons nevertheless captured the attention of the next generation of inventors all over Europe who had better ideas for making them longer, lighter and more manageable for single shooters on foot or horseback.

REPRODUCTION U.S. CARRONADE CANNON with 42-inch, 300-pound cast-iron barrel. This type of cannon was used by the military and Merchant Marine during and after the Revolutionary War. It can now be purchased through Dixie Gun Works, Inc.

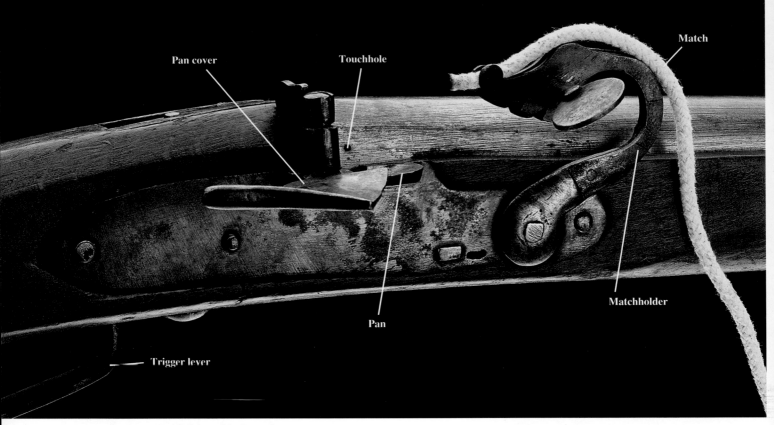

Seventeenth-century English matchlock musket

Muzzleloader Ignition Systems

The entire development of muzzleloader ignition systems is nothing short of human ingenuity working full tilt to bring firepower to black powder as quickly as possible. The following discussion outlines the seven systems – matchlock, wheellock, snaphaunce, miquelet, flintlock, percussion caplock and in-line percussion caplock – to acquaint you with their history and how they work.

Matchlock

The first known illustration of a matchlock firing mechanism appeared in 1411. Matchlock firearms were used initially in Italy around 1450. Over the next 100 years, many variations were devised, but they were all based on the same principle of attaching a serpentine metal cock (matchholder) lever to the barrel of the muzzleloader over a priming pan next to the touchhole leading into the chamber. Early matches were constructed of nothing more than twisted cords, which were more than likely difficult to get burning, let alone keep burning for any length of time. Later matches were soaked in various

solutions of sulfur or saltpeter (potassium nitrate), then allowed to dry. These matches would not only burn better but would also burn for a much longer period of time.

Around 1470, when the shoulder stock was developed, a snapping matchlock system evolved along with it. Derived from the crossbow, a flat metal spring was attached to hold the priming match away from the touchhole until the shooter pulled a release mechanism called a *trigger*.

One of the most advanced matchlock designs was the sixteenth-century Spanish arquebus. The shooter kept his long, smoldering match in a metal perforated tinderbox that hung from his belt. When ready to shoot, he attached the lit end of the match to the cock above the touchhole and filled priming pan. He then shouldered the gun with one arm extended under the carriage and used his other hand to move the pan cover aside and lower the match to the powder.

Even though more sophisticated locks were invented in the sixteenth century, matchlocks continued to be used in Europe until as late as 1700. In 1543, the Portuguese introduced matchlock firearms to Japan, where they were used well into the nineteenth century. While the shooter was able to sight down the barrel of the gun, the matchlock system was frightfully slow and cumbersome. What was needed was an ignition system capable of producing its own fire.

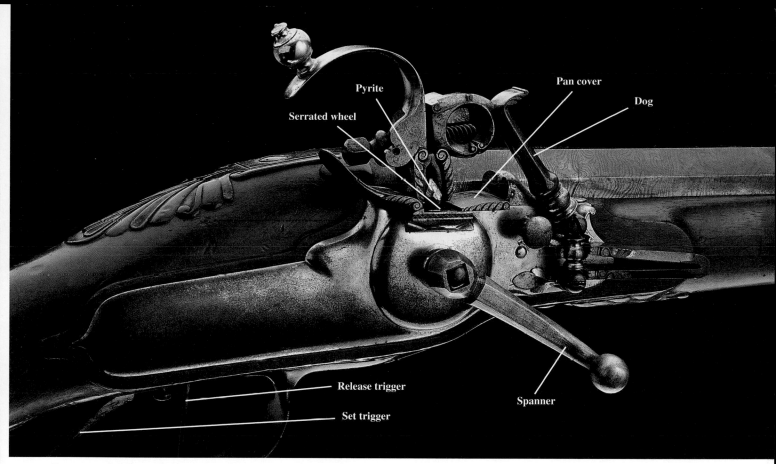

Pyrite

Serrated wheel

Pan cover

Dog

Release trigger

Set trigger

Spanner

Germanic wheellock rifle – eighteenth century

Wheellock

The Florentine artist-architect-sculptor Leonardo da Vinci (1452-1519) made line drawing illustrations of a new wheellock firing mechanism in 1508. Besides his other talents, da Vinci had been civil and military engineer to Duke Lodovico Sforza in Milan since 1482, and his interest in this ignition device was more than passing. It was left to the Germans in the city of Nuremberg to refine the wheellock during the early 1500s.

Although a vast improvement over the matchlock, in that the fire could be self-made on site, the wheellock did have its pros and cons. The advantages were that it was often lighter; more manageable to prime, aim and fire; and less affected by weather, because its workings were internal. Wheellocks were the first mechanized firearms to be widely used on horseback with lead bullets, and the firing mechanism was a natural to be adapted to the pistol when it emerged around 1540.

The main disadvantages, especially for military use, were that it was very expensive to produce and the complexity of its mechanism made it vulnerable to breakdown. In addition, the Spanish Pope banned wheellocks in the Holy Roman Empire in 1518 – a move surely designed to keep the matchlock playing

field level in the never-ending conflicts of the sixteenth century. Wheellock firearms became the rich man's muzzleloader.

The wheellock system relied on a piece of iron pyrite, which was held against the surface of a serrated steel wheel by the dog, or cock, of the lock, positioned on the breech of the barrel facing backward. The wheel was wound by a spanner (wrench), until it was locked in place by a sear (pin) and other workings of the lock mechanism. Powered by a mainspring, the wheel spun when the trigger was pulled, and the contact of the pyrite to the serrated wheel created a shower of sparks. Between the wheel and barrel was the flash, or priming pan, which contained a tiny amount of fine black powder. The sparks from the friction of the pyrite and wheel ignited the priming charge. The flash found its way through a small vent leading into the bore, where the main charge was detonated.

The importance of the wheellock as a transitional firing system was twofold: it did away with smoldering matches and it had a sliding pan and wheel cover that automatically moved out of the way when the trigger was pulled. These features meant that the gun could be primed, cocked and ready to fire in advance.

By the mid-1500s, an unknown inventor in northern Europe came up with a design that took the wheellock's pyrite-and-wheel friction device to the next (but simpler) level of lock development.

Snaphaunce

Derived from Dutch, the word "snaphaunce" has a colorful background that gives clues to why the name may have been chosen for the first flint-and-steel muzzleloader lock system. "Snap" meant to bite with the jaws. "Haunce," was the word for a rooster or cock that had a distinctly dangerous beak. The two words together meant "snapping or vicious cock." In the late 1500s "snaphaunce" in northern Europe was also the name for an armed robber or highwayman – could it be that these notorious thieves brandished a particularly ingenious type of quick-firing pistol? "Snaphaunce" describes perfectly the jawed cock that thrusts the flint against the steel on these sixteenth-century smoothbore muskets and handguns.

The earliest documentary evidence of the snaphaunce lock is dated to 1547. Reversing the forward position of the wheellock's cock mechanism to the rear and using flint instead of pyrite, the snaphaunce also replaced the serrated wheel with a tempered steel blade called a *frizzen*. Gripped in the jaws of the cock, the flint swung in a forward arc powered by the mainspring of the lock. As it struck the face of the frizzen, particles of steel were scraped away and heated by friction, which resulted in a shower of sparks. The sparks fell into the uncovered priming pan below the frizzen, igniting the powder. The flash from the powder traveled through the vent hole, detonating the main charge.

On early models, the frizzen operated separately from the cover of the pan, so that the shooter had to manually open the pan and put the frizzen in place. On later versions of the snaphaunce, the pan cover was mechanically moved by the cock falling against the frizzen. Besides the important innovation of the flint-and-steel fire source, the snaphaunce was far easier and cheaper to produce than the wheellock because its simple external mechanisms were more accessible than the complex internal workings of its forerunner. The Dutch-style snaphaunce was widely adopted in Algeria and other parts of North Africa down to the nineteenth century.

About the same time the snaphaunce gained favor in northern Europe, another lock system similar to it was developed in the south – ironically, it also was named for a band of roving thieves.

Miquelet

A member of a gang of Catalonian bandits active in the Pyrenees mountains between Spain and France in the late 1500s was called a *Miquelet*. The new quick-firing ignition system for muskets and pistols adopted the name from these armed mountaineers.

Exhibiting a jawed cock identical to the snaphaunce and utilizing flint and steel in the same manner, the miquelet contributed significant improvements that

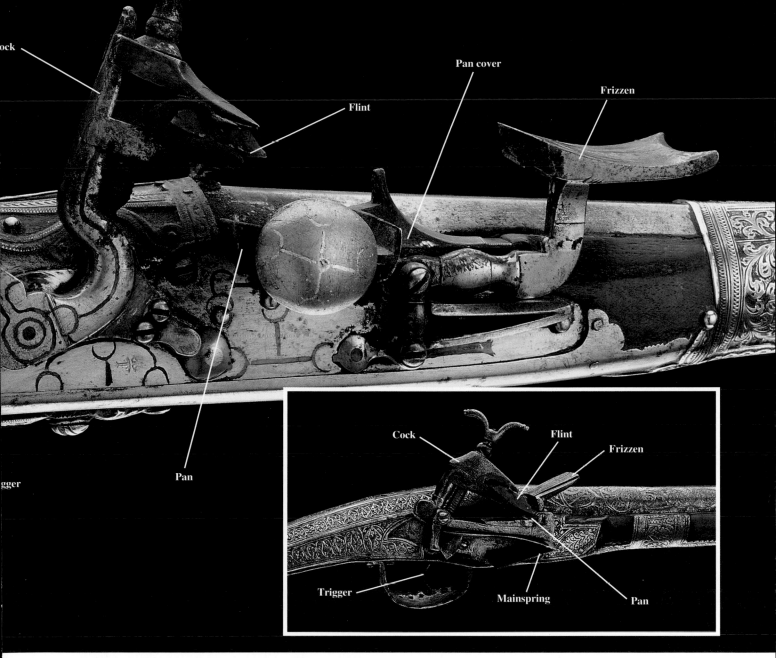

ock

Flint

Pan cover

Frizzen

Pan

gger

Cock

Flint

Frizzen

Trigger

Mainspring

Pan

Mediterranean snaphaunce musket and Mediterranean miquelet pistol (inset)

made ignition more mechanical and faster. The frizzen and pan cover were made in one piece, and the cock could be held to half- or full-cock with the aid of an external mainspring and metal support called a *bridle*. When the trigger was pulled, the flint arched forward, striking and pushing back the frizzen, thus exposing the priming pan below. The time between pulling the trigger and throwing sparks into the pan was greatly reduced.

Most miquelet lock systems featured internal mechanical parts, but like the snaphaunce, several miquelets had these parts on the exterior. Miquelet

muskets were preferred in the Mediterranean and Balkan regions up to the nineteenth century.

The combination of the snaphaunce and miquelet innovations led to the invention of the true flintlock muzzleloader. The introduction of this much-improved ignition system and the growing use of bores with rifling were to receive worldwide acceptance by early muzzleloading hunters. Military forces throughout Europe were quick to make the switch to the flintlock musket, but the rifled bore remained a luxury for the sportsman until well into the nineteenth century.

Flintlock

Trigger

The flintlock is believed to have been developed in France around the turn of the seventeenth century. It incorporated the best features of the flint-and-steel snaphaunce and miquelet systems and also internalized and mechanized more of its parts. When the Pilgrims landed at Plymouth Rock in 1620, they brought with them an array of early muzzleloading firearms, which may have included wheellock and flintlock smoothbore muskets among the more common matchlock guns.

Arms experts generally accept the flintlock as the first "practical" muzzleloader ignition system. Frontloaders built with the flint-and-steel ignition system allowed the shooter to carry the arm loaded, primed and ready to shoot – with reasonable certainty that the gun would, indeed, fire when the trigger was pulled. The flintlock was without question the worldwide number one muzzleloader for 2 centuries, until the early 1800s.

The mechanics of even the finest original flintlocks and modern reproductions are relatively simple. The external components include the hammer (cock), flash pan, frizzen and frizzen spring. The hammer has three parts: the hammer proper, the top jaw and the top jaw screw. The top jaw grips the piece of flint. The flash pan sits forward of the hammer and features a shallow trough for holding a priming charge of exceptionally fine black powder. The frizzen is connected to the front of the pan and also acts as a cover when flipped rearward in the closed position. The frizzen spring is commonly attached to the lock plate and provides the necessary tension to keep the frizzen securely closed over the pan.

All of these parts work together to achieve ignition. As the trigger is pulled, the hammer falls forward,

causing the sharpened edge of the flint to strike the heat-treated hardened surface of the frizzen face. As the hammer continues forward and downward in its arc swing, the flint scrapes away at the frizzen. The force results in tiny particles of steel being scraped away by the sharp edge of the flint and falling in the form of sparks into the now exposed priming powder in the pan. A very small amount of the resulting flash finds its way through a tiny vent hole in the

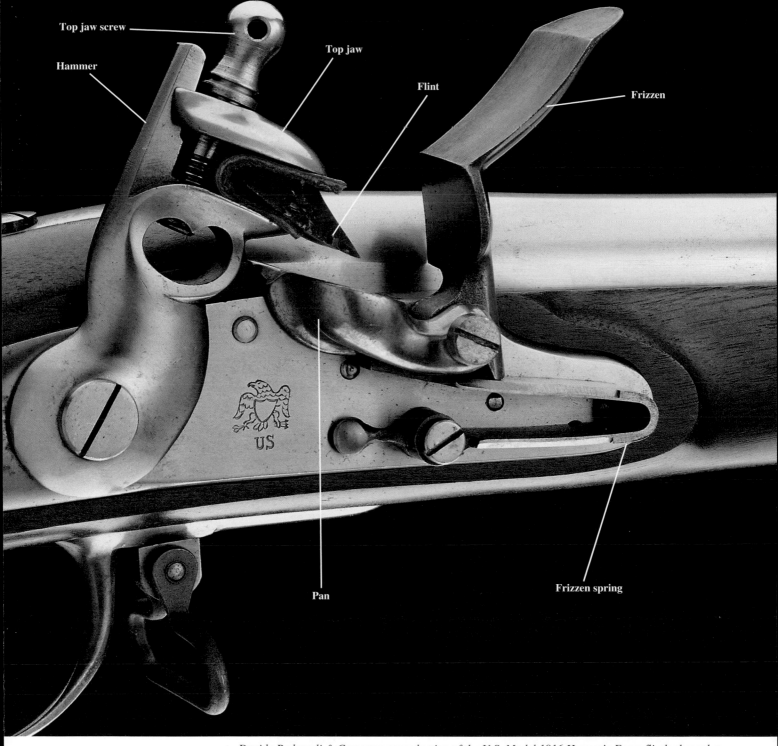

Top jaw screw

Top jaw

Hammer

Flint

Frizzen

US

Pan

Frizzen spring

Davide Pedersoli & Company reproduction of the U.S. Model 1816 Harper's Ferry flintlock musket

side of the muzzleloader's barrel and finally ignites the main powder charge.

The common trait of the matchlock, wheellock, snaphaunce, miquelet and flintlock is that the fine black powder priming mixture is held on the outside of the gun. Wind and wet weather wreak havoc on filled priming pans and fire sources. Even if enough grains are left for a match or a shower of sparks to

ignite the primer, the flash is often too weak to reach the main charge in the barrel.

The possibility of surefire ignition would only come from a system that generated a spark within the gun itself. The discovery in the late 1700s of a new priming explosive that could be used in firearms was the impetus behind the development of the percussion caplock system.

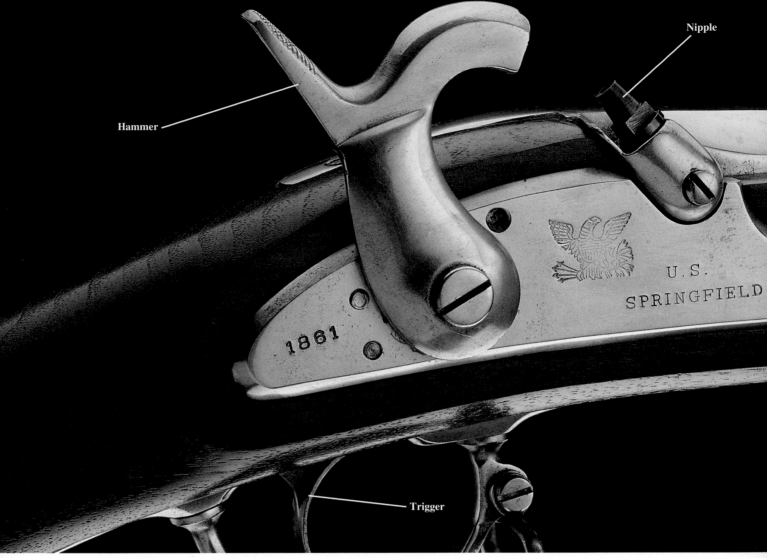

Hammer

Nipple

1861

U.S.
SPRINGFIELD

Trigger

Dixie Gun Works, Inc.'s reproduction of the 1861 Springfield percussion caplock rifled musket

Percussion Caplock

Fulminates – shock-sensitive salts of fulminic acid – were discovered to have explosive properties in the 1700s. French King Louis XV's chief physician reported on his findings concerning fulminate of mercury in 1774, but these were not yet applied to firearms. In 1799, however, an Englishman, E. C. Howard, mixed fulminate of mercury and saltpeter together, making a substance called *Howard's powder.* Although fulminates are highly explosive, Howard's powder proved to be relatively stable. Seven years later, a Scotsman used fulminates to create a spark inside the combustion chamber of a gun for the first time.

Reverend Alexander John Forsyth (1768–1843), a sportsman and amateur chemist from Belhelvie, of

Aberdeenshire, Scotland, was unhappy with the way the flash from black powder in the pan of his flintlock scared wildfowl before the main charge ignited. He remedied this problem by developing a system that offered spontaneous, surefire ignition. It was called *percussion* because the new fulminate priming substance had to be hit, rather than lit, in order to ignite.

After several years of experimenting, and total rejection by the military, Forsyth applied for and received a patent on his idea. With the assistance of James Purdey – later to become renowned in the manufacture of fine, high-quality firearms – Forsyth set up business at No. 10 Piccadilly, London, in 1808. His first percussion ignition system was a scent-bottle design. This system relied on a bottle-shaped container attached to the side of the barrel. To prime, a small round charge of fulminate was dropped inside and a plunger was then attached to the bottle. The hammer struck the plunger, detonating the fulminate, which in turn ignited the main powder charge.

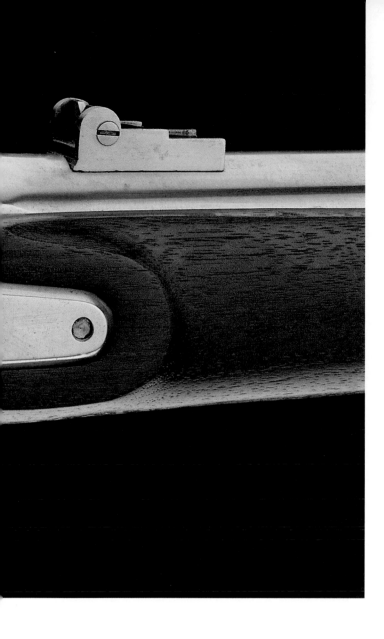

A percussion cap is a small copper cup about $\frac{1}{8}$ inch in length and diameter (right). It is open on one end, and a minute amount of fulminate of mercury is placed on the inner surface of the closed end.

In use, the cap is placed over a short hollow tube, called a *nipple.* The nipple is threaded either into the barrel or a shoulder attached to the barrel. When struck by the hammer, the fulminate inside the cap fires and the resulting explosion is directed to the powder charge through a flash channel that runs through the nipple and into the barrel. Even early percussion caplock systems gave the shooter instant ignition that was somewhat immune to the effects of damp weather, hang-fires (delays in ignition) and misfires (failures to ignite).

The switch from the flintlock to the percussion caplock ignition system was the swiftest in the evolution of the muzzleloader. In a matter of 30 years, percussion ignition had all but replaced the 200-year-old flint-and-steel system. Around the world, ingenious gunsmiths devised easy ways to convert flintlock arms to percussion.

During the same period during which fulminates replaced fine black powder as a primer and the percussion caplock overcame the flintlock, smooth-bored barrels likewise gave way to rifled bores. German gunmakers came to America during the late 1600s and early 1700s with the knowledge of cutting spiraling grooves that ran the inside length of the barrel. Originally, it was thought that these grooves would collect the fouling left from a burning powder charge and make loading succeeding shots much easier. It was also discovered that the grooves helped stabilize the patched round ball projectiles and improved accuracy at longer ranges.

Military minds of the time were slow to change, and the switchover from flintlock to percussion military arms didn't take place until nearly a quarter of a century after the percussion ignition system had been perfected. European and American armies had nearly universally adopted the percussion ignition system by the early 1840s, and the rifled bore became more and more commonplace. Twenty years later, these rifled muskets became the standard firearms for both the North and the South in the American Civil War.

By the time the Civil War broke out in 1861, the percussion ignition system had been thoroughly refined. The large-bored percussion rifled muskets of both

Later versions, known as *pill locks,* located the ball of fulminate in a shallow trough next to the barrel, similar to the pan of a flintlock. The flash from the explosion of the fulminate had to enter a vent hole in the side of the barrel, much like the flash of a flintlock's priming charge, resulting in many of the same problems that hampered the older ignition system. There were other versions of the percussion ignition system, but all basically operated in the same way: the blunt nose of the hammer struck and exploded the charge of fulminate.

By 1820, the cap element of the system was perfected. Although there has been some controversy over just who actually developed the true percussion cap, and whether it was developed in Great Britain or in the United States, by the early 1820s rifles and pistols utilizing the more efficient ignition system were being built in both countries. The percussion cap operated on a simple principle and, with its reasonably reliable firing capability, won worldwide acceptance.

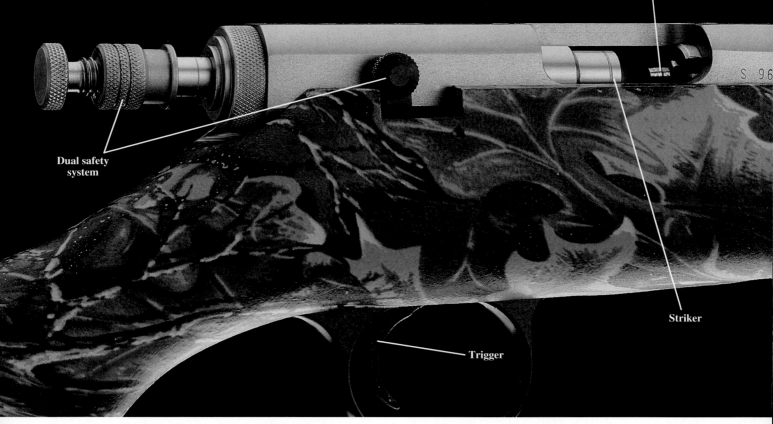

Dual safety
system

Striker

Trigger

Knight Rifles MK-85 Predator in-line percussion caplock

the North and South relied on winged musket caps which produced two or three times as much fire as the smaller sporting percussion caps.

The Civil War is often referred to as "the last of the old wars." It was certainly the last of the major conflicts in which muzzleloaders played a significant role. Even before the outbreak of hostilities, much had already been done to develop the breechloading, self-contained cartridge – a tubular container that combined priming, powder and projectile in one unit. Consequently, the bloody battles of the war became the proving grounds for this next step in firearms development. Repeaters such as the Spencer and Henry established their effectiveness through the sheer volume of fire they produced. During an early demonstration for the Army Ordnance Department, the Spencer sustained a rate of fire of 21 rounds per minute for an extended period and fired a total of 250 rounds without a stop to clean the repeater. Even the best rifled musket could not do this.

Although there were many gunmakers who continued to make quality percussion sporting guns following the development of cartridge firearms, the percussion era was one of the shortest in muzzleloader development. However, from its refinement in about 1820 until its

heyday during the late 1850s and early 1860s, many distinguished percussion sporting arms were produced in the United States, Great Britain and Europe. From this era came names such as Hawken, Manton, Purdey, LePage, Billinghurst and Whitworth, who have been honored among the finest gunmakers of all time.

The search for the ultimate percussion muzzleloading ignition system continues even today. Inspired by the great numbers of big-game hunters wishing to participate in special muzzleloader seasons, a thoroughly modern seventh ignition system made its debut in the mid-1980s.

In-Line Percussion Caplock

In 1985, gunsmith William "Tony" Knight perfected the in-line percussion caplock ignition system. Early configurations of the in-line ignition system have been around since the early 1700s. Several elaborate German-built in-line flintlock guns are known to exist and have been dated to the 1720s. There were also several early in-line percussion ignition system guns dating from the early 1800s, shortly after the percussion cap had been perfected. The extremely close tolerances required to house a hammer inside a receiver were nearly impossible for gunmakers of those periods, and original in-line ignition muzzleloaders are among the rarest of the rare.

The modern in-line percussion ignition system designed by Tony Knight features a plunger-style hammer, or *striker*, which is cocked by pulling it straight to the rear. When the trigger is pulled, the hammer slams forward to strike a percussion cap on the nipple, which is positioned directly in the rear center of the breech plug. Fire from the exploding cap reaches the powder charge the instant it leaves the nipple.

In addition to spontaneous, surefire ignition, the modern Knight ignition system provided today's hunter with a rifle equipped with a safety system, much like that found on a modern centerfire hunting rifle. The receiver also allowed for easier mounting of a scope to aid accuracy, and the design of the removable breech plug provides the shooter with a muzzleloader that is easier to clean and maintain.

In 1996, Remington Arms Company took in-line percussion muzzleloader development to a new level with the introduction of the company's revered Model 700 bolt-action centerfire rifle in an all new muzzleloading configuration. The Model 700ML retains many of the features of the popular cartridge model, including a modified bolt with a flat faced striker (hammer) for faster lock time than possible with a plunger-style in-line rifle hammer. And with a special plastic "weather shroud" in place at the face of the bolt, this gun is nearly 100 percent weatherproof.

Ruger, Connecticut Valley Arms, Traditions, Knight and a new firm known as Austin & Halleck quickly followed the introduction of the Remington muzzleloader with a tremendous selection of "bolt-action" muzzleloaders. While these latest in-line ignition frontloaders may vary slightly in design and cosmetics, all feature a bolt-type hammer that does speed up lock or hammer time considerably, and all are built with bores that feature a fast 1-turn-in-24 to 32 inches rate of rifling twist for improved accuracy with modern saboted bullets.

Muzzleloading continues to evolve into a true hunting sport, and it is now more performance driven than at any other time in history. The majority of today's shooters are hunters, and nostalgia ranks low on their lists of reasons why they picked up the sport. These muzzleloader fans are looking for improved, faster and more surefire ignition, better 100-yard accuracy, and a rifle that delivers a well designed projectile with the authority to cleanly down big game. Today's new breed of in-line ignition rifles, many of which now rely on shotgun or rifle primers for ignition, are delivering that performance.

Reproduction Muzzleloaders

The scarcity of fine old original muzzleloading guns in safe shooting condition can be credited for the introduction of modern-made reproductions. Although today's serious antique arms collector wouldn't think of putting irreplaceable original muzzleloaders through the rigors of everyday shooting, black powder fanciers of the 1930s, 40s and early 50s had little choice. Once these guns were lost to use and abuse, they were lost forever.

The reproduction, or replica, muzzle-loading firearms we enjoy today can be attributed to two men who had the foresight to see the need for strong, well-built modern copies of original frontloaders. Turner Kirkland (right), a west Tennessee gun collector, founded Dixie Gun Works and began marketing the first

Turner Kirkland

reproduction muzzleloading rifle in 1955. That rifle was the .40-caliber Dixie "Squirrel Rifle," a Belgian-manufactured copy of a typical Kentucky longrifle of early 1800s styling. The rifle was first offered in Dixie's 1956 catalog in a choice of flint or percussion ignition at $79.50.

The other early pioneer in the reproduction muzzleloader industry was Val Forgett of Navy Arms Company. In 1958 the newly formed company imported the first modern copy of the Colt 1851 Navy revolver from Italy. During the Civil War, this .36-caliber percussion revolver was one of the most copied and remains one of the most recognized cap-and-ball revolver designs dating from the heyday of percussion wheelguns. Navy Arms' replica of this famous handgun was so exact that it created a dilemma for beginning arms collectors who could not distinguish between a heavily used and worn Italian-made copy and an original Colt revolver from the mid-1800s.

From the success of these two guns has grown an entire muzzleloading industry, with a selection of guns that now includes contemporary copies of many flintlock and percussion models dating from the 1700s and 1800s.

Some modern day black powder shooters are fascinated with muzzleloading designs from the past. Occasionally, a custom gunsmith will totally hand-craft an authentic copy of a European matchlock or wheellock. But most of today's shooters limit interest to muzzleloaders with flint or percussion ignition. This is because the selection of well-built reproductions has never been better.

Muzzleloading Equipment

Flintlock Long Guns

Shooting and hunting with a flintlock muzzle-loader represents the ultimate challenge for today's black powder shooter. Mastering such an early "external" ignition system requires nerves of steel. Most shooters can't resist the urge to flinch when the priming powder in the pan "whooshes" right in front of their eyes. Then, there's the seemingly long delay from the time the pan ignites until the muzzleloader actually fires. Yet, it's impossible to pick up a faithful copy of an original flintlock rifle or smoothbore musket without wondering what it must have been like to rely on such firearms for protection or to put food on the table.

Even though the sale of flintlock guns represents less than 10 percent of the muzzleloaders sold today, the selection of quality flint and steel muzzle-loaders is still outstanding. The muzzleloading shooter looking to relive a little history can

choose from such guns as the Dixie Gun Works Tennessee Mountain Rifle, the Pedersoli 2nd Model Brown Bess smoothbore musket, or the Traditions Pennsylvania Rifle. These are just a few of the several dozen different flintlocks currently being made.

In Pennsylvania, a state with a very strong muzzle-loading tradition, hunters partaking in the annual white-tailed deer muzzleloader season can use **only** flintlocks. In addition, only patched round balls (p. 47) and open iron sights are legal during this special muzzle-loader hunt.

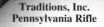

**Traditions, Inc.
Pennsylvania Rifle**

**Davide Pedersoli & Company
2nd Model Brown Bess Musket**

**Dixie Gun Works, Inc.
Tennessee Mountain Rifle**

Percussion Long Guns

It is doubtful that Tennessee gun collector Turner Kirkland had any idea of the industry he was starting when he introduced the first reproduction muzzleloading rifle back in 1956. His Dixie Gun Works .40-caliber Kentucky rifle may have seen only about 20,000 of the rifles sold, but it spawned an industry that has since produced millions of muzzleloading guns, the vast majority of which have been of percussion ignition.

Easily 90 percent of the muzzleloaders sold today feature a percussion caplock or in-line percussion caplock ignition system. The selection presently available includes quality-built modern copies of full- and half-stocked big-game hunting rifles, long-barreled squirrel rifles, Civil War rifled muskets and elaborate target rifles. At one time or another since the first reproduction muzzleloader appeared during the mid 1950s, there has been a modern copy of just about every percussion longarm originally produced.

Percussion Caplock Long Guns

One model stands out as the best-selling muzzleloading sporting rifle of all time: a contemporary copy of the famous Hawken rifle.

Only the big .58-caliber Springfield rifled muskets of the Civil War were produced in greater numbers than the Thompson/Center Arms Hawken, which was first offered in 1970. To date, more than 1 million of the modern half-stock rifles, rifle kits, and variations of the Hawken have been purchased.

Percussion caplock rifles are being produced by almost all of the muzzleloader manufacturers in calibers suited for hunting any species of game. Left-hand models are also readily available. Some of the latest rifles sport durable, composite stocks and stainless steel barrels designed to perform in the harshest weather conditions.

Thompson/Center Arms Co., Inc.
Hawken

Thompson/Center Arms Co., Inc.
Grey Hawk

Connecticut Valley Arms, Inc.
St. Louis Hawken Classic

In-Line Percussion Caplock Rifles

The number one apprehension of the muzzleloading shooter is whether or not his frontloader will fire when the trigger is pulled. After all, improved ignition is what drove muzzleloader development through the ages. Shooters have long recognized that the more instantaneous the ignition, the better the chances of hitting the target with accuracy. The in-line percussion caplock ignition system answers these concerns.

For the most part, the new breed of muzzleloading shooters couldn't care less about historic design. Instead, hunters want a rifle that can deliver optimum performance on deer and other big game. That kind of performance is now possible, thanks to significant design changes. Some of today's new in-line muzzleloaders can perform on par at 100 yards with many out-of-the-box centerfire hunting rifles.

More than any other rifle, the Knight Rifles MK-85 changed how the serious big-game hunter looks at muzzleloading. Designed by gunsmith William "Tony" Knight in 1985, this in-line percussion frontloader bears little resemblance to the long, heavy and awkward muzzleloading rifles of traditional side-hammer design. In fact, the Knight MK-85 displays all the classic lines of a fine bolt-action centerfire sporting rifle, not to mention the handling characteristics and safeties of a modern firearm. Plus, with the proper loads, the Knight MK-85 is a muzzleloader capable of producing $1\frac{1}{2}$-inch groups at 100 yards.

Through the 1990s, in-line percussion rifles accounted for the majority of all muzzleloader sales. Due to the popularity of the Knight rifle, other manufacturers like Thompson/Center Arms, Traditions, Connecticut Valley Arms and Lyman added at least one in-line hunting rifle to their line, and by the end of the decade big gun makers like Remington and Ruger were also catering to this market with improved bolt-action designs.

Whether the guns feature the plunger-style hammer of the original Knight design, or a faster bolt-style hammer, such as that found on the Remington and Ruger muzzleloaders, today's more popular in-line rifles share many common features. Thanks to relaxed hunting regulations across the country, scopes are now allowed during most muzzleloader big-game seasons. To make it easier for the shooter to install a scope, practically all in-line rifles now come with the receiver already drilled and tapped for scope base installation. A remov-

able breech plug is also now standard on most all in-line rifles, making it easier to give the rifle a thorough cleaning and to remove an unfired round without having to shoot the rifle. Manufacturers have also recognized the individual tastes of muzzleloading shooters and now offer a mind boggling selection of wood, laminated and composite stocks, with many models available with a standard or thumbhole grip. Most guns are also available in a choice of blued or stainless steel barrel.

Connecticut Valley Arms, Inc.
Apollo Dominator

Knight Rifles
MK-85 Predator

Traditions, Inc.
Buckhunter Pro

Thompson/Center Arms Co., Inc.
Fire Hawk

Knight DISC Rifle

Muzzleloading into the 21st Century

When looking at the very modern lines and experiencing the equally impressive performance of in-line percussion rifles like the Remington Model 700ML and the Ruger Model 77/50, it may seem that muzzleloader development has gone just about as far as today's designers and manufacturers can take it. Still, for the most part, these futuristic-looking frontloaders continue to rely on the good ol' standard No. 11 percussion cap or slightly larger winged musket cap for providing the fire that ignites the powder charge. In other words, as modern as these guns may appear, they still rely on an igniter that is basically the same as the one used nearly 200 years ago.

New Muzzleloader Designs

The continued desire for a hotter, more reliable and sure-fire ignition system has recently resulted in a number of new muzzleloader designs built around an ignition system that utilizes either modern No. 209 shotshell primers or center-fire rifle cartridge primers for providing the spark that gets everything moving down the barrel. And these primers do put considerably more fire into the powder charge. In fact, one study has shown that a large rifle primer is good for nearly 10 times the fire possible with a No. 11 percussion cap, while the No. 209 shotshell primer delivers upwards of 15 times the amount of fire produced by one of the small percussion caps. The shotshell primers also produce about 5 times the amount of fire generated by the best winged musket cap.

During the late 1990s, Knight Rifles introduced a "bolt-action" in-line ignition rifle known as the Knight DISC Rifle. Just as the model designation suggests, this rifle incorporates a plastic disc that holds a No. 209 shotshell primer. Once the rifle has been loaded and is ready to be "primed," the bolt handle is lifted upward. This causes the bolt to cam rearward slightly, and exposes a priming port at the face of the bolt. One of the primed plastic discs can then be very easily dropped into this opening, and as the bolt handle is pushed downward, the bolt cams forward, compressing the plastic disc between the face of the bolt and the breech plug.

When the trigger is pulled, fire from the shotshell primer shoots through a tiny orifice in the breech plug to the powder charge on the other side. Ignition is extremely fast and positive.

Primer DISCs and No. 209 shotshell primers

An added bonus of so much fire to the powder charge has also been better initial ignition and more complete consumption of heavier hunting charges, which means slightly better velocities and energy levels. Knight Rifles was one of the first muzzleloader manufacturers to promote the use of three 50-grain Pyrodex pellets (150-grain charge) behind a saboted bullet for magnum muzzleloader performance with the DISC Rifle. So loaded, this rifle is capable of spitting out some saboted bullets at more than 2,000 f.p.s., with energy levels approaching that of a modern center-fire rifle.

Not to be left out in this latest round of muzzleloader development, Thompson/Center Arms now offers a uniquely styled "break open" muzzleloader they have dubbed the Encore 209x50 Magnum—a rifle they tout as "The Most Powerful .50 caliber Muzzleloader in the World!" Here is another very modern frontloader that has been designed and built to shoot hefty powder charges consisting of three 50-grain Pyrodex pellets. And for ignition, this rifle also relies on super-hot No. 209 shotshell primers.

Thompson/Center Encore 209x50 Magnum Rifle

The action of this rifle operates the same as Thompson/Center's line of single-shot center-fire pistols. When the shooter pulls upward on a spur at the rear of the trigger guard, it releases the barrel lock and the gun opens up very much like Grandpa's ol' single-barrel shotgun. Instead of a nipple, the breech plug features a tiny recess, or chamber, for inserting one of the shotshell primers once the rifle has been loaded. And when the action is closed, this ignition system is totally protected from foul weather.

With a three 50-grain Pyrodex pellet load behind a saboted 240-grain jacketed hollow-point bullet, the company claims that the 26-inch barreled Encore 209x50 Magnum muzzleloader is good for 2,203 f.p.s. at the muzzle. This translates into 2,577 ft. lbs. of big-game taking energy, or about the same as a .30/06 with a 150-grain bullet. The company offers the gun in a 15-inch barreled handgun model as well.

Millennium Designed Muzzleloaders currently offers a similarly designed .50-caliber rifle, handgun and 12-gauge muzzleloading shotgun built on a break open action. These frontloaders come standard with a breech plug designed for use with No. 209 primers. However, the company offers an optional breech plug for use with either No. 11 percussion caps or the larger, winged musket caps.

The Lenartz Rdi-50 is another "new wave" muzzleloader designed and built for use with the hotter No. 209 shotshell primers. What sets this rifle apart from anything else that utilizes a No. 209 primer is its very unique and efficient ignition design. The Rdi-50 ignition system consists of three major parts—a specially engineered breech plug, a rotating chamber or ignition cover, and a short-throw plunger-style hammer.

Once the rifle has been loaded, it is one of the easiest to prime. First, the hammer is cocked rearward and locked into place by sliding the handle upward into a safety slot in the receiver. The ignition cover is then opened by lifting upward on a small handle, exposing a priming port. A No. 209 primer is then dropped into the opening, and the ignition cover handle is pushed downward. This causes the cover to cam forward, holding the primer in place against the rear of the breech plug. Once the rifle is fired, the hammer is cocked back, the ignition cover opened, and the spent primer is easily dumped out. The Rdi-50 features a very simple, yet efficient ignition system that puts a great amount of fire into the barrel.

Connecticut Valley Arms, Markesbery Muzzle Loaders, and a few other muzzleloading manufacturers also now market big-game frontloaders that are fired with modern primers. While better, more surefire ignition is partially the reason for the switch from percussion caps, better game-taking performance with magnum powder charges has been the real reason for these hotter ignition systems. All of these rifles have been built to handle a load consisting of three 50-grain Pyrodex pellets.

The Latest Innovation

Well, as hi-tech as these ultra-modern systems may seem, there is currently an entirely new muzzleloading concept available that is sure to change this 700 year old shooting sport one more time. The rifle and ignition system concept are the brainchild of North Carolina custom gunsmith Henry Ball.

What makes this frontloading system so different than anything else that's ever been offered is that here, at last, is a muzzleloader specifically designed, engineered and built to be shot with SMOKELESS POWDER!

That's right, a muzzleloader that can be safely loaded and fired with smokeless powder loads, which are cleaner burning, non-corrosive, more economical to shoot, and better performing than traditional black powder or Pyrodex. The designer of this system felt that since the modern muzzleloading hunter has been continually striving to get his frontloader to perform more like a modern center-fire hunting rifle, why not build one that will? The result is a very user-friendly frontloader capable of amazing accuracy and knockdown power.

The heart of Ball's custom smokeless muzzleloader has been a modern center-fire rifle action. He has built the hot frontloaders on a wide range of actions, including everything from surplus Remington rolling-block actions, to Ruger No. 1 actions, and even on a Winchester Model 94 lever-action—turned into a single shot muzzleloader. Still, he favors the good ol' bolt-action for building a rifle with tack-driving qualities.

This maker has been custom crafting the rifles one at a time since the mid-1990s, and it was just a matter of time before a major gun maker took notice of this very superior muzzleloading system. Today, Savage Arms Inc. has brought to the shooting public Ball's advanced muzzleloading technology at about one-fifth the cost of his original custom rifles.

True to Henry Ball's patented design, the new .50-caliber bolt-action Savage Model 10ML features a breech plug that chambers a

Percussion module and No. 209 shotshell primers

reusable steel "percussion module," which can be easily primed with a No. 209 shotshell primer using just thumb pressure. When the bolt of the Savage Model 10ML closes behind one of the primed modules, this system is fully weatherproof and puts 100 percent of the fire from the primer through the tiny .030-inch orifice in the breech plug and into the barrel.

The very precise fit of the module in the chamber of the breech plug also totally eliminates the escape of gasses and pressure. In fact, when a module is removed from a fired rifle, the outside surfaces are totally free of any fouling, whether this rifle was fired with black powder, Pyrodex or a prescribed smokeless propellant. And it is this precise fit, plus the strength of a modern bolt-action receiver, that allows this muzzleloader to be fired with smokeless powder loads.

The hot, three 50-grain Pyrodex pellet loads fired in newer models from Knight, Thompson/Center, and others already covered in this book generate in the neighborhood of 15,000 to 18,000 p.s.i. inside the barrel. The smokeless loads that perform so well out of the Savage Model 10ML produce chamber pressures in the 40,000 p.s.i. range, which will completely destroy any other muzzleloader.

One of Henry Ball's favorite saboted bullets is the 300-grain .45-caliber Hornady XTP jacketed hollow point, loaded into the .50-caliber Savage barrel with a Muzzleload Magnum Products high-pressure sabot. With a precisely measured 45-grain charge of IMR 4227, the bullet leaves the muzzle of the 24-inch Savage barrel at about 2,250 f.p.s., and with an unbelievable 3,370 ft. lbs. of knockdown energy. This is about the same energy level produced by a 7mm Remington Magnum. Amazing!

Even more impressive is the downrange performance of this rifle and smokeless loads. Sighted 2-inches high at 100 yards, the aforementioned load prints just 2 inches low at 150 yards, and barely six inches below point of aim at 200 yards. Out of the same rifle, a three 50-grain Pyrodex pellet load sighted in the same manner prints about 4 inches low at 150 and a full foot low at 200 yards. Out at 200 yards, the 45-grain charge of IMR 4227 delivers the 300 grain Hornady with about 1,800 ft. lbs. of game stopping knockdown power.

Cleaning any of the other muzzleloader designs has always been a major apprehension among shooters looking at muzzleloading for the first time. The thought of having to thoroughly scrub corrosive fouling from the bore and other parts after every shooting session has kept many from ever getting into muzzleloading. Now, here is a muzzleloader that requires no more cleaning and maintenance than any modern firearm.

In the past, names like Turner Kirkland, Val Forgett, Warren Center, and Tony Knight brought innovations that have had a profound impact on the sport of muzzleloading. Following in their footsteps, Henry Ball is a new frontloading genius sure to help shape the future of muzzleloading as we head into the 21st century.

SAFETY CAUTION: Do not attempt to load and shoot any smokeless propellant (other than Pyrodex) out of any other muzzleloader than the Savage 10ML. No other muzzleloader currently available has been built to withstand the higher pressures.

Savage Model 10 ML

Knight TK 2000 Shotgun

Shotguns

Muzzleloading shotguns are basically offered in two forms – those having just one barrel and those having two barrels. A number of companies that import from Italy and Spain offer modern copies of the English side-by-side percussion doubles, which were once used world-wide by wingshooters. Many of the doubles presently available display excellent lines and balance and are a delight to take afield.

A few double- and single-barrel shotguns have been designed specifically with today's turkey hunter in

mind. These guns easily handle the magnum powder and shot charges needed to hunt these large birds. In fact, most of the single-barrel turkey shotguns and a couple of the double-barrels are built with removable extra-full choke systems that deliver very tight patterns for quickly killing gobblers at distances up to 40 yards. A few in-line percussion models are available with durable composite stocks for years of dependable use in tough hunting conditions.

And, finally, for the flintlock fan, there are a couple of early *fowlers*. For the most part, these smoothbores are available in the popular 12-gauge, but a couple of 20- and 10-gauge models are presently offered as well. The hunter who chooses to enter the duck or goose blind carrying one of these guns has accepted one of the toughest challenges in bird hunting.

Davide Pedersoli &
Company Mortimer
Shotgun

Davide Pedersoli &
Company Magnum
Double-Barrel
Shotgun

Pistols

Frontloading handguns are available in a wide variety of models, which generally fall into one of two different classifications – of the muzzleloading single-shot variety, or of the multi-shot percussion revolver design. The selection currently available easily covers more than 200 years of handgun development.

The muzzleloading single-shot pistol is an appropriate companion sidearm to many flint and percussion long guns. Today's shooter can choose from flintlock or percussion models that range from early flintlock English belt pistols to late percussion "Hawken"-style handguns of the same caliber as the big-bore rifle being carried. **And for the modern muzzleloader fan, some in-line percussion pistols, like the Thompson/Center Encore 209x50 Magnum Pistol, feature a removable breech plug and the power to warrant their use on deer and similarly sized big game. This particular frontloading handgun**

Thompson/Center Encore 209x50 Magnum Pistol

will consume upwards of 110 grains of FFg black powder or Pyrodex, thanks to hotter No. 209 shotshell primer ignition.

The percussion wheelgun fan will find a tremendous offering of six- and five-shooters available. Some of the more popular guns include modern copies of the .36-caliber Colt 1851 Navy Model, .44 Colt 1860 Army Model, .44 Remington "New Model" Army, .45-caliber Ruger "Old Army" and many of the so-called "Pocket Model" percussion revolvers.

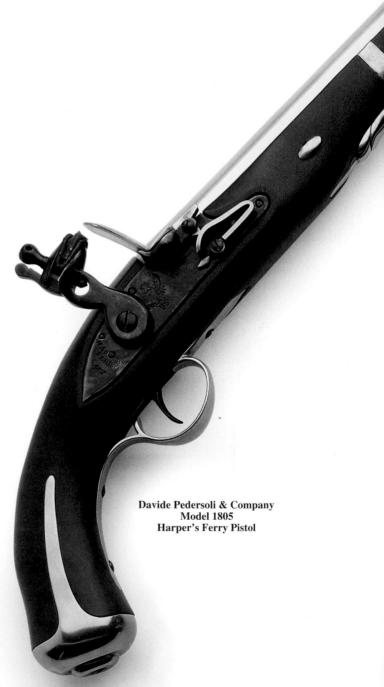

**Davide Pedersoli & Company
Model 1805
Harper's Ferry Pistol**

Traditions, Inc.
Buckhunter Pro

Dixie Gun Works, Inc.
Colt 1851 Navy

Traditions, Inc.
1863 Pocket Remington

Handmade Muzzleloaders

The very fact that a person turns to muzzleloading indicates that he or she is looking for a break from the norm. Within those ranks are the truly dedicated charcoal burners who want to stand out from the crowd even more by owning a frontloading gun that is different from what is readily available off the dealer's shelves. Building a rifle from a kit, assembling a muzzleloader from component parts or contracting a custom muzzleloading gunsmith to build a truly "one-of-a-kind" piece of art offers many that escape.

Muzzleloader Kits

Kits for building a muzzleloading rifle, pistol, musket, shotgun or even a cap and ball revolver, have been popular since the early l970s. At one time or another, just about every manufacturer or importer of black powder guns has offered kits of their best-selling guns. There are a number of reasons why these kits have been so popular with today's shooter, but the main reason is that black powder burners tend to enjoy having a hand in the making of the frontloaders they shoot. They take pride in carrying a muzzleloader that's a little different from what everyone else is shooting, and like to say, "I built it myself!"

With care and attention to detail, it is possible for the kit builder to turn one of today's mass-produced kits into a muzzleloader with much better looks than the same gun finished by the manufacturer. The really talented builder can turn out a gun that looks like a true custom muzzleloader, with more refined stock contours and authentic finish than the same rifle, mass-produced by the factory.

Muzzleloader kits do not necessarily save money, however. When you consider the price of the kit, then add other costs such as sandpaper, steel wool and finishing products, most kits don't represent much of a savings over a factory-finished rifle. For example, to purchase a kit for a rifle that retails for about $300 factory-finished, you'll pay about $200. Add to that the cost of everything you'll need to finish the gun, and you've increased the cost of the project another $30 to $40. Then, if you decide to have the barrel or other metal parts professionally hot-blued, you may find that you've spent as much or more on the kit than if you had just purchased the finished gun.

Fortunately, most of today's kits don't require a great deal of gunmaking skill to assemble and finish. Lock inlets, barrel channels, cuts for the trigger guard and buttplate, along with the drilling and tapping of all holes in the metal parts are usually already done. Many of the kits also include prefinished barrels and locks. On these kits, the builder is mostly a stock finisher and assembler. Yet, all kits allow makers to add personal touches that instill a feeling of pride in having had a hand in the construction of the muzzleloaders they shoot.

It's not unusual for the first-time kit builder to try to build a project that's too advanced for his capabilities. Without any knowledge of muzzleloader systems, the novice should stick to one of the easier kits to assemble. These offer a challenge to someone who has never shaped and finished a stock, made minor inletting adjustments or prepared metal parts for finishing. Early success engenders confidence, and, as a rule, confidence leads to a better job at completing a kit. With patience, most first-time builders can produce quality workmanship with one of the easier kits. Once the builder has assembled and finished two or three of these, he is ready to move on to a more challenging kit project.

Keep in mind that you get what you pay for. A major mistake made by many first-time buyers is to purchase the cheapest kit possible. When you see a kit that retails for about half the price of other similarly styled kits, the lock, trigger and barrel are often of lesser quality. No matter how much time you spend making the muzzleloader look attractive, you still have a cheap frontloader when you complete the project. Kits that do not function properly, after the builder has spent countless hours fitting and finishing all of the parts, have discouraged many black powder shooters from ever attempting to build another.

Choosing a Kit

Before buying a kit, check it thoroughly. Make sure the kit contains all the parts needed to complete the project. Missing parts that require calling the factory for replacements can delay the project for weeks, or even months.

The three major components you should inspect most closely are the lock, the stock and the barrel. If any are of poor quality, the appearance or the performance of the finished kit will suffer. Therefore, it is best to choose a brand-name kit that's backed by a good reputation.

Many dealers will allow you to unpack a kit and inspect the parts. However, some won't, because many kits are now "blister-" or "heat shrink-"

Tips for Choosing a Kit

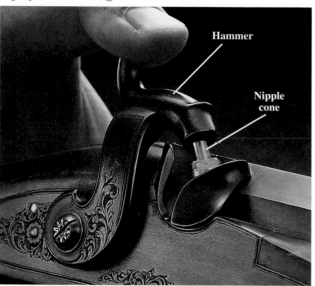

CHECK preassembled percussion caplock kits for correct alignment of the hammer with the nipple. The nipple's cone should be nearly centered in the shallow recess of the hammer's nose (above).

INSPECT preassembled flintlock kits to be sure the vent hole in the barrel is just above the top center of the pan (above). If the vent hole is positioned too low, it will fill with priming powder and lead to slow ignition.

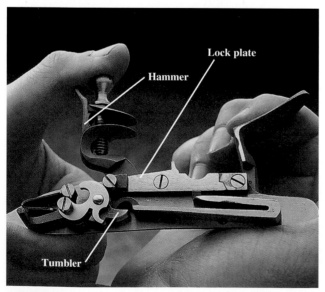

TEST the smoothness and positiveness of the lock mechanism. A binding of the hammer against the lock plate, or the tumbler against the inside of the lock plate, indicates poor quality.

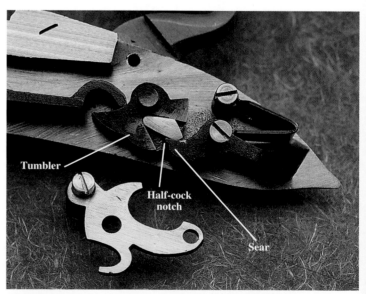

EXAMINE the kit's lock to make sure the tip of the sear readily pops into the full- and half-cock notches of the tumbler (above). If the sear fails to engage both of these notches, the lock is unsafe.

packaged in a special plastic film, making repackaging all the parts next to impossible. When buying a kit that has already been opened, inspect it closely to make sure that all the parts are there. If you're buying a kit from a dealer who won't allow you to open it, or if ordering from a mail-order firm sight unseen, again, stick with a brand name.

Most kits are accompanied by a complete set of building instructions. It usually takes about 8 to 12 hours to finish and assemble one of the easier muzzleloader kits.

Building a muzzleloading long gun or pistol from a kit is an enjoyable activity that helps to pass away those otherwise idle winter hours. The one quality that the kit builder will find to be an absolute necessity is patience. All the kit-building talent in the world is wasted if you don't have patience with your muzzleloader project.

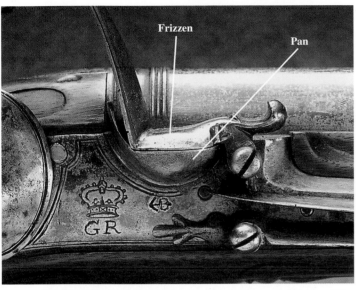

SNAP a flintlock's frizzen shut over the pan. On a quality lock, the frizzen should fit closely to the pan (above). If it doesn't, moisture can easily get to the priming charge or wind can blow the fine priming powder out of the pan.

TEST the stock with your thumbnail. If moderate pressure leaves a mark (above), the finished stock will dent easily. Kits with softwood stocks sand and shape easily, but they are not as strong as maple or walnut hardwood stocks.

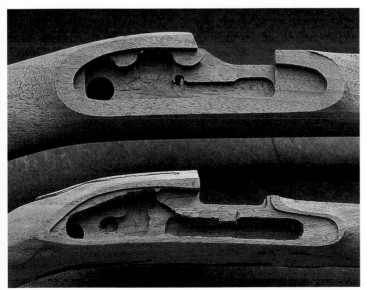

LOOK for clean inletting cuts in the stock (top). If they are frayed (bottom) you may end up with loose-fitting inlets. Tight-fitting inlets can be enlarged for a better fit, but inletting that starts out too big results in a sloppy fit of parts.

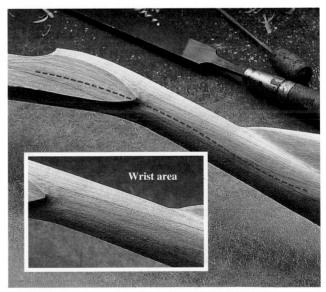

CHECK the wood grain in the wrist area of the kit's stock (inset). For the strongest possible stock, the grain should follow the slight curve through the muzzleloader's wrist area (dotted line above).

KIT-BUILDING TOOLS AND SUPPLIES include: (1) flat and round files, (2) wood and metal finishes, (3) checklist of kit parts, (4) sandpaper in successive grits, (5) inletting chisels and (6) whetstone for sharpening the chisels. Having everything handy at the outset allows you to concentrate on your project without interruption.

Kit-building Tips

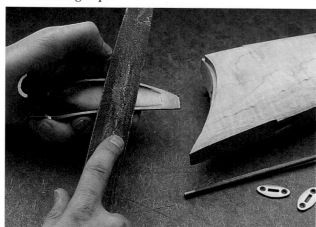

FILE or sand the kit's buttplate (above), trigger guard or other metal parts if they do not fit the stock's factory inlets. Do this before removing any wood from the stock. This will result in an overall better wood-to-metal fit.

SHAPE the stock and the metal parts flush whenever possible. File from wood toward metal to avoid contaminating wood pores with fine grains of metal, which might discolor finished woodwork.

WRAP a round file with sandpaper to add a little style to the contours of a cheekpiece (above), or to the area around the lock. But use caution – any wood removed from the stock is impossible to put back.

USE a sanding block and not your fingers to power the sandpaper back and forth on the stock. This prevents the wavy surface that often results from sanding with uneven finger pressure. Always sand with the grain of the wood.

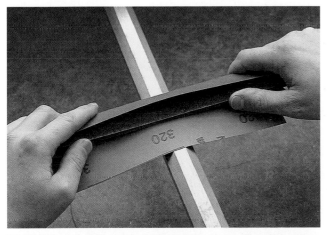

POLISH an octagonal barrel by wrapping a flat file with fine sandpaper and carefully drawing down the flats. Make sure the file rides the surface squarely. Wrap the file with a good medium-grit emery cloth for final polishing.

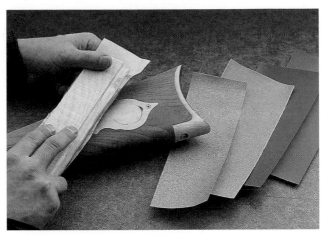

BEGIN sanding the stock with the coarsest grade of sand-paper needed to get the job done, usually 80-grit. Next, move to a finer 120-grit paper. Finish up with a really fine 320-grit paper.

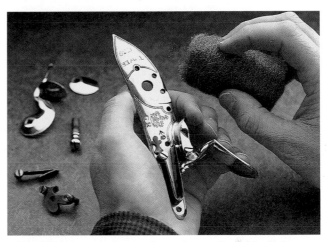

REMOVE the metal parts from the stock and buff them with OOOO grade steel wool after first polishing them with a superfine, 400-grit, wet/dry type sandpaper. All of the brass parts are completely finished at this point.

CHOOSE wood and metal finishes that best compliment your frontloader. Many muzzleloader kit builders prefer traditional metal finishes such as worn patina (top), or dark (cold rust) brown (bottom).

Custom-Made Muzzleloaders

The decision to contract a well-known, custom gunmaker to build a truly one-of-a-kind frontloader is a major step for any black powder shooter. Let's take a look at what you get for your money when purchasing a custom muzzleloader.

Even when custom gunmakers use commercially available parts, most rely on the very best. Some of the locks currently available are almost exact duplicates of the finest locks dating from the past. These feature internal surfaces that have been highly polished, and a precise fit between parts for smooth, trouble-free operation. It's not unusual for some of these locks to carry a higher price tag than most complete muzzleloader kits.

The barrels are generally the highest-quality cut-rifled barrels available today. They are produced by pulling a cutter through the bore to remove a very small amount of steel with each pass. To cut a typical eight-groove, rifled barrel with .006- to .010-inch-deep grooves requires from 150 to over 200 passes of the cutter. These precision-cut barrels are time-consuming to produce and extremely accurate.

Many of the more complicated custom rifle designs are built with a swamped barrel, modeled after original American longrifles of the late 1700s. Swamped barrels feature a large, ouside-diameter muzzle, then taper to a smaller diameter toward the middle, then flare back out to a larger diameter at the breech end. Many of these barrels measure over 40 inches in length, which makes it easy to understand why their cost is generally higher than most reproduction rifles.

As you might guess, the finest locks and barrels are installed on the highest-quality woods available to the custom gunmaker. Not many shooters will contract to have built a truly "Plain Jane" design from the past. Even when a less ornate gun is ordered, it's usually

built with fine wood. High-grade curly maple and nicely figured walnut command a premium price. This is especially true for a piece of wood that's long enough to full-stock a rifle that might feature a barrel of 40 inches or more. Relief carvings in the wood and brass or silver inlays (right) also add to the beauty of a custom gun's stock.

Relief carving and silver wire inlay

Although the old term "lock, stock and barrel" is often used to characterize something that includes everything, it takes a lot more that just these three parts to complete a fine custom muzzleloader. The buttplate, sideplate, trigger guard, nose cap, ramrod thimbles, trigger, sights, patchbox and toe plate are some of the other parts needed to build most custom muzzleloaders. Many of today's finest riflesmiths totally handcraft these features. Those makers who purchase some or all of these items, generally do so from a craftsman specializing in these parts for the custom muzzleloader trade.

Depending on the complexity of the style being re-created, a custom gunmaker may spend 80 to more than 400 hours building a muzzleloader just the way you want it. Today's makers are producing some of the finest muzzleloaders ever built. The availability of locks and barrels allows gunmakers to concentrate effort on the production of a stylish frontloader, rather than on the time-consuming task of making these parts. In addition, these parts are now made from higher-quality steels than were available in the past.

Most gunmakers require a considerable deposit before accepting an order. As a minimum requirement, it's not uncommon for a builder to ask for the cost of parts with the order. This might be anywhere from $400 to $1,000. While prices for custom muzzleloaders vary greatly depending on the maker, you can expect an exceptional, custom-crafted muzzle-loading rifle to cost $2,000 to $4,000. As investments, fine custom muzzleloaders have increased in value, as makers have become known and collectible.

Then, there's the delivery time. A year or more is fairly typical. Some of the better gunmakers are more than 3 years behind on orders. One advantage of such a long delivery time is that it will allow you to pay the balance on the gun more conveniently.

Barrel engraved with gunmaker's name

If you are thinking about investing in a fine custom muzzleloader, be sure to choose a reputable maker (left). This will give you peace of mind that your money is being well spent and that the end product will be a treasure to own.

A FINE .50-CALIBER FLINT LONGRIFLE by Joseph Scorsone of Asheville, North Carolina, in the style of Isaac Haines, Lancaster County, Pennsylvania, circa 1770. This trim longrifle is stocked in curly maple, decorated with rococco carving and inlaid with silver wire. The brass parts have a dark patina finish, with flat facets to reflect the octagon theme of the barrel. Steel surfaces are rust-browned to a dark chocolate nonglare matte finish.

Projectiles

Patched round ball

Prior to selecting a particular style of muzzleloader, first determine exactly the type of projectile you intend to shoot. Black powder shooters basically have four projectile types that can be loaded and shot from a muzzleloading rifle: patched round balls, elongated conical lead bullets, modern saboted bullets and shot loads (below). As a rule, sabots have the flattest trajectory of the muzzleloading bullets, followed by conicals and round balls (p. 52).

It takes an entirely different muzzleloader to obtain optimum performance with either a patched sphere of lead or a heavy conical bullet. The key to accuracy lies in the rifling found in the bore.

Since the 1970s, a number of manufacturers have offered rifles with bores featuring lands and grooves that spiral with a 1-turn-in-48-inches rate of twist. This means that a projectile completely spins once in 48 inches, its "rate" of twist. (It does not mean that the barrel is 48 inches long.) The guns have barrels of 26 to 32 inches long; the most common length is around 28 inches.

This rate of twist was touted as the ideal for obtaining good accuracy from the same rifle, with both a patched round ball and an elongated conical bullet. Rarely, however, did one of these rifles produce the desired accuracy with both types of projectiles.

MUZZLELOADING PROJECTILES are available in four types: (1) round balls, (2) conicals, (3) saboted bullets, and (4) shot loads.

Patched Round Balls

The best accuracy with a patched round ball is achieved by a muzzleloader that has a "slow" rate of rifling twist. True round ball barrels are commonly rifled with grooves that spiral with 1-turn-in-60 to 66 inches; some even feature slower rates of twist.

Keep in mind that accuracy with a patched round ball is the result of a projectile being spun by rifling that the projectile itself never touches. The role of the patch is to grip both the soft lead ball and the grooves of the rifling (above). Because the patch plays such a critical role in round ball accuracy, the material it is made of is very important.

Experienced round ball shooters tend to prefer patching material with a very strong, fine, tight weave. The material must stand up to (1) considerable compression as the ball is being loaded into

RECOVERED PATCHES should **not** show the following: (1) burnt holes, (2) a burnt ring around the circumference area of the ball (3) or slits in the material. An ideal patch (4) should have a blackened spot where it contacted the powder charge, light streaks where the material compressed into the rifling, and a circular ring where the ball flattened when fired to form a very tight seal of the patch and ball with the rifling.

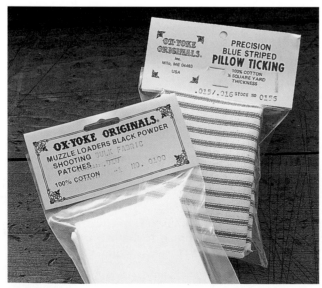

PATCHING MATERIAL for shooting round balls must have a tight weave and be very strong. Most shooters prefer a fabric made of 100 percent cotton.

the barrel, (2) tremendous heat when pushed back down the bore by the burning powder charge, and (3) a great deal of friction when being loaded and eventually shot down the bore at velocities exceeding l,500 f.p.s. Patching material that tears during loading or upon ignition, or that is easily burned through by the powder charge, will never give the shooter acceptable accuracy.

Recovered patches (above) can tell a shooter a great deal about the material being used, the load being fired and even the quality of the rifling in the bore. If there is a spot that's burned all the way through the patch where it made contact with the powder charge, the material is likely too thin. If there is a burnt ring around the circumference area of the ball, it could mean that the ball-and-patch combination fits the bore too loosely. Slits in the material could mean one of three things: either the ball-and-patch combination fits the bore way too tightly; the material is being cut by rifling with overly sharp or rough edges; or abrasive rust deposits have appeared in the bore due to poor cleaning habits.

Ideally, a recovered patch should display a slightly blackened spot (but not burned through) where it made contact with the powder charge. You should see light streaks where the material was folded and compressed into the grooves of the rifling. There should also be evidence of a circular ring where the soft lead ball flattened upon ignition to form an even tighter fit of the ball and patch with the rifling. When your recovered patches look like this, you're using the right ball-and-patch combination.

Gunmakers of the 1700s and 1800s often provided their customers with a round ball mold for the rifles they built. Back then many of the barrels were hand-reamed and rifled; no two bores were exactly alike. They could be .42-, .48-, .52-, or some other odd caliber. To ensure good accuracy with the rifle, makers custom-cut a ball mold for the particular bore.

Very few shooters still cast their own projectiles. Competition shooters who do considerable shooting may cast their own lead balls to save money. Others may own and shoot a rifle that turns in its best accuracy with a ball whose diameter size is not readily available. But most of today's shooters can easily buy the appropriate round balls in a wide variety of diameters.

Most reproduction muzzleloaders feature button-rifled bores. This rifling process compresses the grooves into the steel by hydraulically pulling a hardened "button" through the polished bore. Button-rifled bores rarely have grooves deeper than .005 to .006 inches, leaving little room for compressing a really thick patching material.

Generally speaking, most muzzleloader manufacturers recommend a patching material that has .010- to .015-inch thickness, and a ball that is .010 inch less than actual bore size. This works out to a .310-inch ball in a .32-caliber bore,

a .350 in a .36, a .440 in a .45, a .490 in a .50, and a .530 in a .54-caliber muzzleloading rifle.

Often a shooter will find that a round ball rifle will perform more accurately when loaded with a ball slightly closer to bore size, wrapped in a thinner patch. For example, instead of shooting a .490-inch ball with .015-inch-thick patching, make a switch to a .495-inch ball with .010-inch-thick patching. Also, when shooting a muzzleloader with deep-groove rifling (which may be as deep as .010 inch), heavier .018-inch to .020-inch-thick patching may be needed for best accuracy.

The properly loaded round ball rifle is deadly accurate. For that reason, it is still the most widely used in muzzleloading competition (p. 121). Determining the best ball-and-patch combination for giving a particular rifle accuracy requires that you experiment with a variety of ball diameters and patch thicknesses. Fortunately, suppliers today offer a great selection of patching materials, cast round balls (made by pouring melted lead into molds) and swaged round balls (pressure-formed from cold pure lead). In the loading section of this book, we will detail the most widely used patching lubricants and loading techniques for the best accuracy with a patched round ball.

Even though the patched round ball is capable of amazing accuracy when properly loaded into the right rifle, it falls seriously short in the energy department (p. 91). This is especially true once shots get out to, and slightly past, 100 yards. For that reason, fewer and fewer knowledgeable muzzleloading hunters rely on the round ball for hunting big game. Instead, they choose conical or saboted bullets.

Original bullet molds for Colt Model 1860 Army Revolvers – .44-caliber

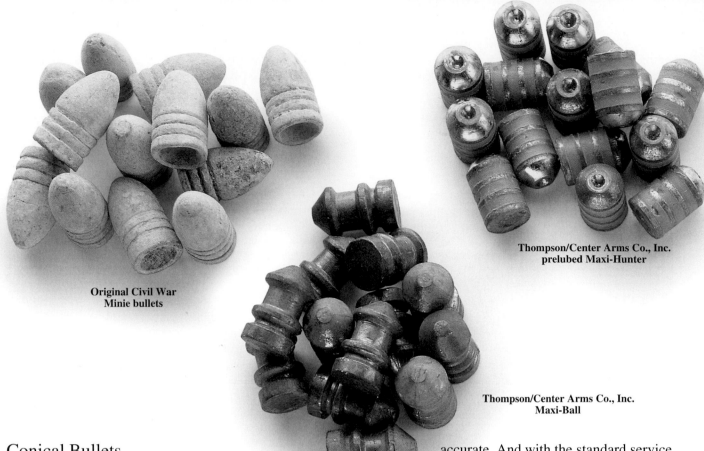

**Original Civil War
Minie bullets**

**Thompson/Center Arms Co., Inc.
prelubed Maxi-Hunter**

**Thompson/Center Arms Co., Inc.
Maxi-Ball**

Conical Bullets

Usually weighing more than twice as much as a round ball projectile for the same-caliber rifle, heavy lead bore-sized conical bullets offer greater energy levels for better big-game knockdown power. However, since these great hunks of lead do weigh so much, it often takes a considerably heavier powder charge to get them out of the muzzle at acceptable velocities.

Conical muzzleloading projectiles first saw widespread use during the 30- to 40-year span preceding the Civil War. A number of unique designs were introduced as hunters looked for a more effective projectile to use on larger game. Some of the earlier elongated muzzleloading bullets are often referred to as sugar-loaf bullets, or picket bullets. The configurations of the various designs were as varied as the different designers' imaginations.

The famed hollow-based Minie bullet of the Civil War was favored for two reasons—its tremendous knock-down power on the battlefield and ease of loading. The bullet itself was slightly smaller in diameter than the bore of a .58-caliber rifled musket. The loose-fitting projectile could be easily rammed down a dirty bore during the heat of battle with just minimal pressure on the ramrod, allowing the soldier to keep firing during a lengthy skirmish. The precise fit of the bullet in the bore is created as the pressure of the burning powder charge forces the thin skirts of the hollow base into the grooves of the rifling. Fired out of the big .58-caliber Springfield and Enfield muskets (issued by the millions), the soft, lead Minie bullets were surprisingly accurate. And with the standard service load of only about 60 grains of FFg black powder, the huge 500-grain slugs would hit with enough energy at several hundred yards to knock an enemy soldier completely off his feet.

Connecticut Valley Arms currently offers a very modern version of the Minie bullet they've dubbed the PowerBelt Bullet. Instead of a hollow cavity in the base of the bullet itself, the PowerBelt design incorporates a separate plastic hollow base that literally snaps onto a short cylindrical post in the rear center of the soft lead projectile. The plastic skirt of this base easily expands into the rifling when the powder charge is ignited. *Obturation*, or flattening of the bullet in the bore as the projectile is hit by the pressure of the burning powder charge, results in a precise fit between bullet and rifling.

Today we generally refer to conical muzzleloading bullets as being either the Minie type or the Maxi type. The Minie bullets used by shooters today still feature the hollow-base design dating from the Civil War. Those bullets generally referred to as Maxi are usually of a flat-base design. Both types require lubrication to obtain good accuracy. For convenience, most bullet manufacturers sell prelubed conicals.

Maxi bullets were popularized by the Thompson/Center "Maxi-Ball" (above), which was introduced during the early l970s. This big, heavy lead conical (and other similar designs that followed) relies on slightly oversized narrow bearing bands for a precise fit with the rifling. When loaded into the muzzle of

Buffalo Bullet Company
prelubed Maxi-Bullet

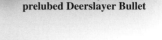

Connecticut Valley Arms, Inc.
prelubed Deerslayer Bullet

Hornady
prelubed Great Plains Bullet

the rifle, the lands of the rifling lightly engrave these soft lead bands. When the powder charge erupts behind the bullet, the base of the bullet still expands to fill the grooves. Both the Buffalo Bullet Company's "Maxi-Bullet" and Hornady's "Great Plains Bullet" are a Minie/Maxi hybrid (above). Both feature a hollow-base design with oversized bands that must be engraved by the rifling during loading.

Because the length of conical muzzleloading projectiles is usually at least twice their diameter, the cylindrical bullets must be spun at a much faster rate to stabilize them in flight. True conical muzzleloading rifles will feature rifling spirals with rates of twist as fast as 1-turn-in-20 to 1-turn-in-32 inches. Also, these bullets are loaded without patching of any sort, so they require relatively shallow rifling for a precise bullet-to-bore fit (right). Rarely will an accurate bullet rifle feature rifling more than .006 inch deep.

There are several benefits to shooting cylindrical bullets from a muzzleloader. First, there is the added energy level for cleaner kills (p. 91). Out of a .50-caliber rifle loaded with 100 grains of FFg, or the equivalent volume of Pyrodex "RS" or "Select," a Maxi-type bullet of 350 to 400 grains will develop about 1/3 more energy at the muzzle than a round ball of 175 to 180 grains ahead of the same powder charge. Also, at longer ranges, the superior design of a conical allows it to better maintain energy. In fact, a heavy conical fired with the load just given will maintain more than three times as much energy at

100 yards than is possible with a patched round ball.

The second benefit of shooting, and especially hunting, with a conical bullet is the speed at which the rifle can be reloaded. The hunter looking to get off a quick second shot will find that most of the newer bullet designs can be loaded more quickly and easily than the patched round ball.

CONICALS fit tightly into the barrel without the aid of patching materials. As a conical is pushed down the barrel, the lands of the rifling engrave the soft lead (inset).

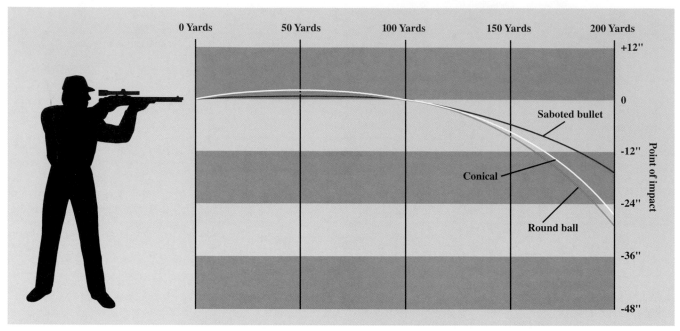

0 Yards	50 Yards	100 Yards	150 Yards	200 Yards	
					+12"
					0
			Saboted bullet		-12"
			Conical		-24"
			Round ball		-36"
					-48"

Point of impact

BULLET TRAJECTORY for saboted bullets is flatter than that of conicals and round balls. As the illustration above shows, a saboted bullet sighted in at 100 yards hits only 1½ inches high at 50 yards and 6 inches low at 150 yards.

Saboted Bullets

A growing number of shooters are discovering that they can get both the accuracy of the patched round ball and the higher energy levels of a heavy lead conical by loading and shooting modern jacketed, or nonjacketed, handgun bullets. The undersized projectiles are loaded into larger-caliber muzzleloading rifles by using a small plastic cup known as a sabot.

The role of the sabot is basically the same as that of the patch when shooting the round ball. Molded from a tough, heat-resistant, space-age plastic material, the base and sleeves of a sabot are easily compressed into the grooves of the rifling as the sabot and bullet are pushed into the bore. The sabot grips both the rifling and the cylindrical sides of the handgun bullet. When the gun is fired, the plastic sabot transfers the spin of the rifling to the bullet as it travels down the bore. Almost as soon as the bullet and sabot leave the muzzle, the sabot falls away and a very modern-design bullet is on its way to the target.

Because the bullet being fired is a cylindrical projectile, the best accuracy with saboted bullets is from rifles with a fast rate of rifling twist. Those muzzleloaders that tend to shoot the bore-sized lead conicals most accurately, generally will produce excellent accuracy with a saboted bullet as well.

Another key to obtaining outstanding accuracy with saboted bullets is to shoot handgun bullets that are close to actual bore size. Today, there are plastic sabots that will allow you to shoot a .357-caliber bullet out

of a .45-caliber rifle, a .40 out of a .45, a .44 out of a .50, a .45 out of a .50, a .44 out of a .54, a .45 out of a .54, and even a .50 out of a .54. Shooters who load and fire a .40-caliber bullet from a .45-caliber rifle, a .45 from a .50, and .50 from a .54 are most likely to achieve the best overall accuracy.

THE PLASTIC SABOT grips the bullet securely as they are pushed into the muzzle. At the same time, the lands of the rifling groove the sabot (inset). When the gun is fired, the sabot transfers the spin of the rifling to the bullet.

| **158-grain**
jacketed .38/.357 Hornady
(.45-caliber rifle) | **240-grain**
jacketed .44 Hornady
(.50-caliber rifle) | **250-grain**
all copper .45 Barnes
(.50-caliber rifle) | **300-grain**
jacketed .452 Hornady
(.54-caliber rifle) | **450-grain**
pure lead .50 Knight
(.54-caliber rifle) |

SABOTED BULLETS are available in sizes and styles suitable for any hunting situation. In general, choose bullets that weigh 240 to 275 grains for deer-sized game and 300- to 400-grain bullets for larger or dangerous game.

Why would a saboted .45-caliber bullet shoot more accurately from a .50-caliber rifle than a saboted .44-caliber bullet? The answer is the thickness of the sabot sleeves (right), which take up the difference between bullet diameter and the larger-caliber bore of the rifle. The thin-

Thin and thick sabot sleeves

ner sleeves of a sabot that encompasses a bullet that is closer to actual bore size will allow the sabot to peel away more quickly once the two have exited the muzzle. The heavier plastic of a sabot surrounding a slightly smaller-diameter bullet will tend to stay with the bullet a little longer and can affect downrange bullet flight.

Sabots are available in several different styles (right). The most popular is the one-piece design. In appearance, this style of sabot looks a great deal like a miniature one-piece plastic shotshell wad. Most feature four thin sleeves that have been designed to peel back quickly once the saboted bullet leaves the

Sabots with four and two sleeves

muzzle. Also, this design features a cupped base that is very similar to the hollow base of the Minie bullet. This allows the thin plastic skirt to expand into the rifling for a better gas seal. Another sabot design relies on two plastic halves that encompass the bullet. To hold these halves in place, a thin felt ring is slipped over the bottom of the sabot. This design also relies on the felt ring to provide the necessary gas seal at the rear of the sabot.

Several years ago, shooters strayed away from shooting sabots because it was rumored that they left a residue of melted plastic in the bore. In fact, several muzzleloading-gun manufacturers even voided their warranties if a shooter fired a plastic sabot out of one of their rifles. Don't believe such rumors. Plastic sabots leave no residue behind, other than the fouling left by the powder charge itself. Millions of saboted bullets have been fired by shooters without any ill effect to the bores of their rifles. Those same gunmakers who once voided their warranties now market saboted bullets of their own.

A number of bullet makers and suppliers market a wide range of saboted lead, jacketed and all-copper bullets. There is a design and weight that is ideal for just about any big-game species you care to hunt.

If, however, you're the kind of shooter or hunter who settles for nothing less than the absolute best load for your rifle, you can also purchase the sabots alone and load with any bullet of the proper diameter. This opens the door to hundreds of different bullet weights, nose designs and construction methods. Speer, Nosler, Hornady, Sierra, Barnes and a number of other bullet makers offer a wide selection of handgun bullets that can be fired from a muzzleloader with a plastic sabot.

The sabot system is the most versatile ever offered the muzzleloading hunter. With .44- and .45-caliber handgun bullets (readily available from around 180 to 400 grains), this system allows today's black powder shooter to specifically tailor his load for the game being hunted (above).

The loading section of this book will cover techniques to obtain the best accuracy with the different types of projectiles. However, always remember that if the bore of a rifle was never intended to shoot a particular style of projectile, all of the experimenting and attention to loading will never make it shoot that projectile. You must decide the type of projectile you intend to shoot before ever buying a rifle.

Shot Loads

Getting a muzzleloading shotgun to pattern a load of shot well enough to take upland game or to break a few clay pigeons has little to do with the type of shot used. For the most part, chilled lead shot is chilled lead shot. Even though a few serious muzzleloading turkey hunters have found that patterns fired with copper-plated lead shot tend to keep a few more pellets toward the center, the shot itself is less important than how the smoothbore is loaded.

A shotgun is not a precision instrument like a muzzleloader with a rifled bore. The fit of the shot load with the bore is not a critical element when loading one of these guns. Keep in mind that muzzleloading shotgun manufacturers of earlier centuries had no concept of choking one of the smoothbores to get tighter patterns. Rather, the approach seemed to be to pour in enough powder and shot to get one of the open-bored shotguns to throw a somewhat acceptable, even pattern at game-taking distances.

Before the introduction of choked barrels, knowledgeable muzzle-loading shotgunners found that the key to good patterns could be found in the sequence of wads stuffed through the muzzle (see Loading with Shot, p. 74).

Another key to good patterns is to load with nearly equal volumes of powder and shot. If a light shot load is placed ahead of a heavy powder charge, the result is normally a huge, open circular area in the center of the shot pattern. This is due to the over-powder card and cushion wad pushing through the shot before falling to the ground. When a heavy shot load is fired with a light powder charge, patterns are usually very sparse, leaving large open areas throughout the pattern

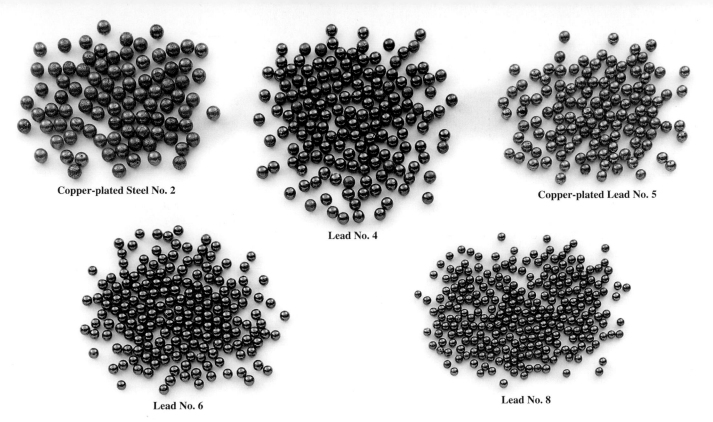

Copper-plated Steel No. 2

Lead No. 4

Copper-plated Lead No. 5

Lead No. 6

Lead No. 8

POPULAR SHOT LOADS (shown actual size) include: No. 2 copper-plated steel for ducks and geese; No. 4 lead for pheasants; No. 5 copper-plated lead for turkey; No. 6 lead for rabbits and squirrels; and No. 8 lead for dove, quail and grouse.

where targets can fly through without being hit by a single pellet.

Some of today's newer muzzleloading shotgun models feature screw-in chokes that produce better patterns, but can make loading a little slower. However, modern chokes do allow the shooter to use a much wider range of loads. With a special steel shot choke tube installed, the muzzleloading shotgunner can even use his frontloader on ducks and geese. One

word of caution: never shoot steel shot through old original muzzleloading shotguns built with soft Damascus steel barrels or through black powder shotguns with chokes designed for softer lead shot.

Later in this book we'll cover specific loads for taking a variety of game with a muzzleloading shotgun. Plus, you'll learn a few tips on how to speed up loading in the field and how to make the muzzleloading smoothbore more weatherproof during those rainy-day hunts.

LOAD with equal volumes of powder and shot to achieve the best possible patterns. A special volumetric shotgun powder/shot measure adjusts for 1- to 1¼-ounce loads.

EXAMINE a load's pattern by shooting at a paper target. A good pattern (above) won't tear a big hole in the center or leave large gaps between the pellets.

Powders

Through the ages, black powder shooters have been faced with determining a proper load of powder for a newly acquired muzzleloader. One approach was to match the caliber of the rifle or smoothbore with a grain-equivalent volume of propellant. This would work out to 50 grains for a .50-caliber, 54 grains for a .54-caliber, and so on. Such loads may have been fine for target shooting, but wouldn't have produced the velocity and energy needed for hunting big game.

If the projectile being loaded and fired was a patched round ball, another approach to determining a starting load was to place the ball in the palm of a hand and cover it with powder until the ball was no longer visible. Then, a powder measure was hollowed out to accept the volume of powder. This approach probably resulted in heftier hunting loads, and likely worked out well with relatively small calibers, from .32 to .50. However, with the really big-bore muzzleloaders such as a .58-caliber or a 12-gauge smoothbore that requires a .710- to .715-inch-diameter ball, this approach would definitely result in "magnum" powder charges exceeding 120 grains.

Fortunately, today's shooter can simply follow the recommendations of the muzzleloader's manufacturer and begin shooting successfully from the very first shots. Although target loads can be much lighter than the suggested hunting loads provided by the manufacturer, never exceed the maximum powder charges recommended.

Before determining just how much powder you intend to load and shoot out of your frontloader, you have to decide which powder you intend to use. Today's shooter can choose from either the modern black powder substitute known as Pyrodex, or the centuries-old black powder formula.

Pyrodex

Pyrodex, currently manufactured by Hodgdon Powder Company, located in Shawnee Mission, Kansas, has been the only successful black powder substitute ever marketed. Introduced by a small Washington State-based company during the mid-1970s, the new muzzleloading propellant was slow, at first, to be accepted by dyed-in-the-wool black powder burners. Today, it is easily the powder most widely used by ever-growing numbers of muzzleloading shooters.

Early supplies of the powder often varied considerably from batch to batch, resulting in inconsistent performance. Since Hodgdon Powder Company assumed the manufacturing of Pyrodex during the late 1970s, the powder has been greatly refined, to the point that many shooters now prefer it over traditional black powder. Pyrodex is offered in several different grades – "CTG" for big-bore black powder cartridge rifles; "P" for muzzleloading pistols, cap and ball revolvers and some smallbore muzzleloading rifles; "RS" for rifles and shotguns; and "SELECT," which is a premium grade of "RS."

Hodgdon Powder Company is also offering Pyrodex "RS" in compressed pellet form, which makes loading many muzzleloaders even easier than ever before. The pellets, offered in various grain sizes, allow the shooter to drop in any combination of the sizes to achieve a desired powder charge. To enhance ignition, the ends of the pellet are coated with a more sensitive igniter, which is easily set off by the flame from a percussion cap. The new pellets perform extremely well in the modern in-line percussion rifles, but due to the long flash channel found in some traditional side-hammer

percussion rifles, ignition isn't always spontaneous; sometimes it doesn't happen at all.

In performance, black powder and Pyrodex produce very similar pressures and velocities. However, each propellant has an up and a down side, forcing you to choose which powder is best for your muzzleloader.

Black powder does ignite more easily than Pyrodex. For that reason, it is the only logical powder to use in a flintlock muzzleloading gun. The flash from the priming powder in the pan simply isn't hot enough to ensure that a Pyrodex charge in the barrel will

Pyrodex Grades
(shown 2¼ times actual size)

"P"

"RS Select"

"CTG"

"RS Pellets"

ignite. Also, those side-hammer percussion guns that require that the flash from an exploding cap travel a great distance before reaching the powder charge will normally fire more spontaneously when loaded with black powder.

The down side of black powder is that it burns so dirty. A single shot with a load of black powder can leave so much fouling in the barrel that it is impossible to load a second shot without first wiping the bore with a damp patch. With each succeeding shot of black powder, this fouling continues to build.

Pyrodex, on the other hand, leaves a very light fouling behind. Many black powder hunters prefer the newer powder because in a field situation they can quickly load a follow-up shot without having to wipe fouling from the bore. Plus, burning Pyrodex tends to consume much of the fouling left from a preceding shot. Built-up fouling is a much smaller problem with the black powder substitute.

Although Pyrodex does burn cleaner, it is harder to ignite and should only be used in those guns with an efficient percussion ignition system. The powder excels in modern in-line percussion ignition rifles.

More and more shooters are now being forced to shoot Pyrodex due to increasing regulations on black powder, which has been classified as a "Class A" explosive. Local, city, state and federal regulations impose strict guidelines on the storage and sale of black powder. Dealers must store the explosive in a fireproof magazine. Pyrodex, however, is classified as a "Class B" flammable solid, the same as modern smokeless powders, and can be stored right out on open shelves. Because most of the muzzleloading shooters they service own and shoot percussion guns, dealers are avoiding the hassle and paperwork associated with black powder, and most now offer only the new Pyrodex.

When working up loads with Pyrodex, always use a volume measure and set it as if using black powder. The new substitute is a bulkier propellant and by actual weight requires about 20 percent less powder to obtain the same velocities and pressures produced by black powder. Pyrodex has been formulated to be loaded on a "volume equivalent" basis with black powder. However, if you were to actually weigh a 100-grain charge of Pyrodex on a powder scale, load and shoot it, you would actually be shooting the equivalent of 120 grains of black powder. Both your accuracy and your shoulder would likely suffer.

Black Powder

The use of black powder as an explosive predates the development of the earliest muzzleloading firearms by several hundred years. There is no written record crediting where black powder was first formulated. However, arms experts tend to agree that the Chinese utilized the explosive before its development in Europe. Still, its refinement as a propellant for muzzleloading guns coincided with the introduction of the first matchlock firearm somewhere in Europe during the late 1300s or early 1400s.

Since its earliest form, the composition of black powder has basically remained the same – charcoal, sulfur and saltpeter (potassium nitrate). Early black powder concoctions were often mixed dry and resulted in ignition that was far less than desirable. During the early refinement of the powder, it was discovered that if these ingredients were mixed using a "wetting" agent, allowed to dry and ground back into granules of a desirable size, the powder allowed for better ignition and produced more consistent accuracy.

The black powder used by today's muzzleloader fancier is the best that has ever been available. Modern manufacturing technology allows powder makers to market a propellant that gives the same performance from can to can.

For the muzzleloading shooter, black powder is generally offered in four different granule sizes, or grades. The finest is FFFFg, which is commonly used as priming powder in the pan of a flintlock. Next is FFFg, which is the propellant charge for smallbore rifles and pistols up to .45-caliber in size. Then there is FFg, which is loaded into larger-bore rifles of .50-caliber or more. And last there is Fg, which is often referred to as "cannon grade" black powder and, as you have probably already guessed, is used to load a muzzleloading cannon. Occasionally a shooter may find that FFg will perform best behind a heavy conical bullet fired from a .40- or .45-caliber rifle, or that Fg works best in a large-bored, .75-caliber musket like the Brown Bess.

Most shooters buy black powder in 1-pound tin cans. Since there are 7000 grains of powder in 1 pound, a shooter can fire 70 shots if he loads with 100 grains each time. Black powder can only be purchased from a dealer possessing a Federal Explosives License.

"FFFFg"

Black Powder Grades
(shown 2¼ times actual size)

"FFFg"

"FFg"

"Fg"

Accessories

Accessories for loading and shooting muzzleloaders fall into two categories: 1) those accessories that are so important to the shooting, loading and maintenance of a muzzleloader that they are considered necessities; and 2) a wide range of accessories that are not essential but may make the sport a lot more pleasurable.

Necessities

One of the most important necessities any black powder shooter can own is a reliable powder measure. Always keep in mind that the key to obtaining optimum accuracy with a muzzleloading rifle begins with the consistency of the loads stuffed in through the muzzle. Those loads begin with a powder charge that's exactly the same from shot to shot. The only way that you can be sure that you're pouring in the same amount of powder for every shot is to rely on a dependable powder measure.

Most of the measures you'll find on today's market are of the adjustable type (below). These will allow you to quickly alter the amount of powder the measure will hold by simply changing the setting and locking it into place. The majority of adjustable measures are a simple tubelike arrangement built with an internal plunger that is pulled down from the bottom of the measure. The farther the plunger is pulled down, the greater the capacity of the measure. Most of these measure as little as 5 grains of powder or as much as 120 grains by volume. Many feature a small knurled

locking screw on the side, which locks the measure at the desired setting. If you own and shoot a variety of muzzleloaders, one of the adjustable measures lets you work up loads for the different guns by simply changing the setting.

If your muzzleloading is limited to just one front-loader, a simple nonadjustable measure is all you need. Muzzleloading shooters of 100 or 200 years ago often fashioned such a measure from a hollowed-out deer antler tine, a piece of wood or even the tip taken from a cow horn. Today's shooter can easily make a nonadjustable measure from an empty cartridge case, a piece of plastic tubing plugged at one end or anything similar that will hold the same amount of powder each and every time when filled level-full. It's still very important to know exactly

How to Use an Adjustable Powder Measure

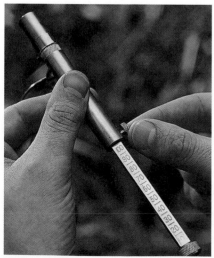

SET the adjustable powder measure to the desired charge.

FILL the powder measure by pressing the spring-loaded valve on the flask.

POUR the powder from the measure into the gun's barrel.

**Mountain State Muzzleloading Supplies, Inc.
Deluxe Powder Horn**

**Traditions, Inc.
Deluxe Flask**

**Thompson/Center Arms Co., Inc.
U-View Powder Flask**

how much powder you're shooting. When you fashion a nonadjustable measure, use either a good balance-beam scale or a quality adjustable measure to determine just how much powder your homemade measure will hold.

The muzzleloading hunter will also need a suitable container for carrying a supply of powder into the field (above). Hunters from past centuries relied on a wide variety of powder horns and flasks for keeping their powder handy...and dry! In Europe, some very elaborate horns or flasks were fashioned from a hollowed-out section of red stag antler or the base from the antler of any other sizable deer. In this country, the American frontiersman tended to favor a powder horn fashioned from a cow horn. Many early powder containers were highly decorated with fancy carvings or detailed scrimshaw patterns and scenes; witty slogans such as "Powder Before Patch and Ball, Or It Won't Shoot At All"; or even a map to help the wilderness longhunter find his way back home.

Early American longhunters commonly packed a sizable horn that held enough powder for an extended

stay in the wilds of the new country. Today's shooter will still find a quality powder horn to be a desirable accessory, especially as a complement to a very traditionally styled Pennsylvania or Kentucky longrifle. For most shooting and hunting needs, however, a horn that holds about a half pound of powder is large enough.

Today's shooters, especially black powder hunters, like to travel lightly. More and more shooters are getting away from packing a large powder horn, relying, instead, on a smaller and handier powder flask. In the past, flasks were typically made of tin, brass or copper; many were decorated with exquisite scenes or patterns similar to those on powder horns. Reproductions of the more popular original powder flasks are currently available from a number of black powder shooting supply houses.

Decoration is less important to today's black powder shooter, who tends to prefer a simpler cylindrical, brass design that has been built to give years and years of service. On the other hand, some shooters prefer a similar flask made of plastic, because of its low cost. Traditional or modern, most flasks will hold between a quarter and a half pound of powder. Most also feature a spring-loaded valve, through which powder is dispensed into a measure. To operate, a lever or button is pushed to open the valve, allowing the powder to flow freely from the container. When the button or lever is released, the valve automatically shuts off the flow of powder.

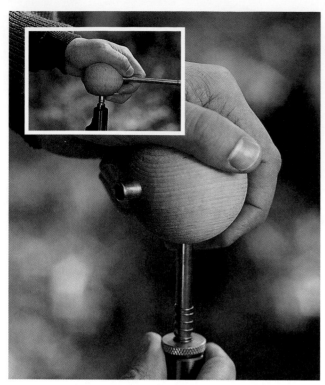

Bullet starter with long (above) and short rod (inset)

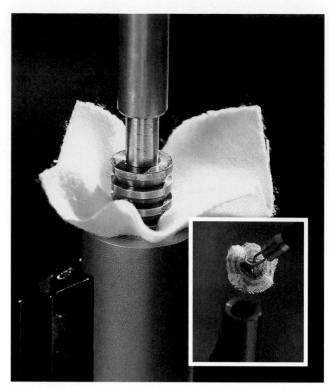

Cleaning jag (above) and patch puller (inset)

When loading and shooting certain projectiles, you'll find that a good *ball* or *bullet starter* (above) becomes a necessity. A properly fitting patch and ball can require quite a push to get the combination through the muzzle and into the bore. This is also true for some modern saboted bullets. Many of the heavy lead conical bullets actually require that the rifling engrave slightly oversized bearing bands when loading. A good bullet starter makes the task of loading these projectiles a lot easier.

Most starters are simple tools with a handle made of wood, metal or plastic, and feature a 3- to 5-inch rod that pushes the projectile into the bore. Some also feature a shorter ¼- to ½-inch rod that is especially handy when patching a round ball with bulk patching. The shorter rod pushes the ball and patching below the crown of the muzzle, which makes trimming the excess patching with a knife much easier.

No matter which projectile you're shooting, a starter allows you to push the projectile several inches into the bore before using the ramrod to push it on down the bore to be seated over the powder charge. A few of the better-designed starters can also be used as an extension for the ramrod, turning it into a more effective cleaning rod.

A dirty bore will destroy the accuracy of the finest muzzleloading rifle barrel. Black powder burns so dirty that a single shot can leave enough fouling in the bore to make loading a second or third shot

impossible. And, even though Pyrodex burns cleaner and allows multiple loadings and shots, accuracy with the black powder substitute is much better when time is taken to wipe the fouling from the bore between shots. A well-fitting *cleaning jag* (above) for the ramrod should be added to a muzzleloading shooter's list of "must have" accessories.

You'll need a cleaning jag for the cleanup at the end of a day's shooting, but you'll also find that your accuracy will improve greatly if you run a damp patch down the bore between shots to keep fouling from building up. Be sure to use a cleaning jag designed for the caliber of your rifle. There isn't much difference in the diameter of a .50- or .54-caliber cleaning jag, but if a .50-caliber jag is used in a .54 rifle, the patch can fit so loosely that it might slip from the jag and stay in the bore.

A worm, or *patch puller* (inset above), is another accessory that threads into the end of a rifle's ramrod. The worm easily pays for itself the first time you have to use it to retrieve a patch that's stuck down in the bore.

If you happen to be one of the growing number of hunters who shoot a modern in-line percussion muzzleloading rifle, you'll find that a good *capper* (opposite page) is another absolute must. The nipple of an in-line percussion rifle is situated down inside a receiver, making it more difficult to reach with the fingers than the nipple of a traditional side-hammer

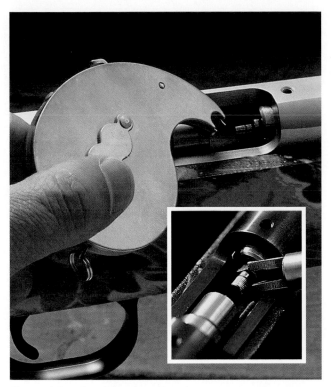

Capper (above) and decapper (inset)

Vent pick

percussion rifle. One of the cappers designed for a percussion revolver also fits down inside the receiver of an in-line percussion rifle and makes it much simpler to place a cap on the nipple. Another nice accessory, a *decapper* (inset above), allows shooters to easily remove caps from the nipple.

All percussion rifle shooters will find that a good capper is a practical accessory to own. When the weather turns cold, it's a lot easier to fit a cap on the nipple of any percussion muzzleloader with a capper than to try to pick up a single cap and place it on the nipple with your fingertips – especially if it's with numbed fingers during a late season muzzleloader hunt. Fortunately, there is a great selection of cappers now available, with a design that's ideally suited for any percussion black powder gun.

If you own and shoot a flintlock, you won't need a capper or decapper. Instead, the flintlock shooter needs a small container for carrying the priming powder. Flintlock shooters of the past often carried a second, smaller priming horn for carrying extra-fine FFFFg priming powder. Many of today's shooters still rely on a small priming horn; others use an accessory known as a *pan primer* (right);

Pan primer

some carry their priming powder in a container as simple as a plastic film canister.

Flintlock shooters should also carry a *vent pick* (above), also called a *nipple pick*, to keep the vent hole clear before priming the pan with powder. Percussion shooters will find this tool handy for making sure the nipple is clear of fouling.

And finally, there is the accessory that the black powder shooter hopes he never has to use, a *ball puller* (right). This tool threads into the bottom of the ramrod and is used to pull out projectiles that have become stuck in the barrel during loading. Shooters can avoid the frustrating process of pulling a stuck projectile by taking a few seconds to clean the bore with a patch between each shot.

Ball puller

These are the accessories that hold the status of necessities. Today's black powder shooter can head for the range or into the deer woods with all sorts of gadgets and goodies filling his pockets or shooting pouch. Or, he can get by with these basic necessities and still enjoy muzzleloading success.

Possibles bags

Other Accessories

So, what are some of the other accessories available for the fully equipped black powder shooter? A shooter's bag, often called a *possibles bag* (above), is a handy pouch for packing around all the gear a black powder burner may find necessary to carry. Such pouches are most often made of heavy leather, but cloth bags were often carried in the past as well.

Also, the shooter who puts quite a few rounds through his muzzleloader may find an *auxiliary cleaning rod* (opposite page) a handy accessory to own. Such rods are often made of a heavy-duty material such as stainless steel or a plastic-coated fiberglass material. Most of these rods have bore protectors to keep the rod centered in the barrel. Auxiliary cleaning rods save wear and tear on the rifle's ramrod, which can be saved for loading and shooting in the field.

Handy plastic tubes known as *speed loaders* (opposite page) are definitely a much appreciated accessory among serious hunters. These convenient arrangements allow the shooter to carry a pre-measured powder charge in one end of the 4- to 5-inch tube,

Speed loader

Knapping hammer

Auxiliary cleaning rod with bore protector

Loading block being filled with patched round balls

then a projectile in the other end. Moistureproof plastic caps snap over each compartment, keeping everything protected from the weather and ready for a quick reload. Four or five of these in a jacket pocket eliminate having to carry a powder flask and measure.

If you are shooting with patched round balls, then you may find a *loading block* (above) another handy accessory. These allow the shooter to carry two or more round balls and prelubed patches that are inserted into holes drilled through a piece of wood. To load one of the balls, all a shooter has to do is align the hole with the rifle's bore and push the patched ball on into the barrel with a short starter. The ramrod is then used to seat the ball over the powder charge.

Flintlock shooters will find a small brass hammer known as a *knapping hammer* (above) a much-used accessory. The tiny, yet heavy, hammer is used to chip away the dull edge of a flint. Keeping a sharp edge on the flint is necessary to ensure good ignition of the priming powder in the pan.

These are just some of the accessories that can and will make the muzzleloading shooter's life more enjoyable. Whether you end up carrying all of these items into the field is entirely up to you. However, just having them around when you need them can make the chore of loading, shooting and cleaning a frontloading gun less troublesome.

Loading & Shooting
Muzzleloaders

Loading Techniques

Drop a measured charge of black powder or Pyrodex down the barrel, seat a patched round lead ball or conical bullet over the powder charge with the ramrod, prime the pan of a flintlock or place a cap on the nipple for a percussion ignition rifle, and you're ready to indulge in some black powder shooting. Sounds like a simple operation, doesn't it? Actually, there's nothing difficult about loading and shooting a muzzleloading rifle, pistol or shotgun, provided the shooter uses the proper components during the loading process. Even then, the manner in which these components are applied can make a big difference in how well the frontloader performs.

Previously, we discussed the powders available, choosing the right powder for specific calibers, and the variety of projectiles available to today's muzzleloader fancier. In this section, we will outline the steps to take to properly combine and load all of these components to obtain the absolute best accuracy and performance from your muzzleloader.

Loading Basics

Before loading any muzzleloading rifle, make sure the bore is free of any oil or other lubricants left from the last cleaning. If the rifle is a brand-new muzzleloader, remove the heavy lube inside the barrel. (This is added by the manufacturer to ensure a rust-free bore if the rifle is placed in a dealer's storage area for any length of time.) Removal is accomplished by running a dry, clean patch down the bore, using just the rifle's ramrod with a cleaning jag threaded into one end. You may also want to use a patch that's been lightly dampened with a good cleaning solvent (right) to cut the heavy lube, which often coats the rifling.

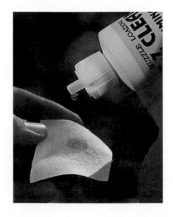

Once lubricants have been removed from the bore, it's time to make sure that the ignition system is clear. With a flintlock, this is simply done by making sure that the vent hole leading from the pan into the bore is free of obstruction. Use a small-diameter wire known as a *vent pick*. Since the vent hole is a straight-in port to the bottom of the bore, there aren't any turns or hidden corners in the vent hole for oil or any other obstructions to block the flash from the pan. Pushing the vent pick through the hole several times will ensure that it is clear (below).

Cleaning a flintlock's vent hole

If the rifle is a percussion muzzleloader, either a traditional side-hammer model or one of the more modern in-line frontloaders, you'll need to first snap a couple of caps on the nipple to make sure that the flash channel from the nipple into the barrel is clear. To do this, use the cleaning jag on your ramrod to push a dry patch down the bore and leave the rod and patch sitting at the face of the breech plug (right). Now, snap two or three caps on the nipple. If oil remains in the flash channel of the ignition system, the first cap will throw the lubricant onto the patch rather than into the bore. Snapping percussion caps two and three times burns what little oil remains in the nipple and flash channel. Often, the oil that was thrown onto the cleaning patch is also completely burned by the additional caps. The bore and ignition system are now free of oil, and the rifle is ready to be loaded.

When loading a muzzleloader of any kind, always keep the muzzle angled away from your face and body during loading. Position the butt of the rifle firmly against the ground, and pour in a measured powder charge. Always rely on a separate measure for pouring powder into the bore. Some powder flask or horn designs allow the shooter to use a spout that

SNAP a few percussion caps on a dry patch while leaving the ramrod and attached cleaning jag in the barrel. The patch will have a burn spot (inset) if the flash channel from the nipple to the bore is clear.

will measure out a given powder charge. However, measuring directly from the main powder container is dangerous. A tiny burning ember from a previous shot, or one left from snapping caps on a percussion gun, could ignite the powder charge as it is being poured into the barrel. If you're holding a flask or horn with as much as a half pound of powder inside, you're holding a potential bomb in your hand. Pouring the powder into a measure, then into the barrel, eliminates the chance of serious injury due to accidental detonation of the powder during loading.

Loading the Patched Round Ball

The round ball is probably the oldest muzzleloading projectile still being shot. During the early development of the first muzzleloaders, projectiles of iron, brass, bronze and stone are known to have been used. Accuracy was basically unheard of until someone discovered that very uniform projectiles could be cast from soft, pure lead. The first of these projectiles was a simple round sphere, which had to be patched in some fashion to produce the absolute best accuracy.

We have earlier covered the importance of loading and shooting the appropriate-diameter round ball and the use of patching material with the correct thickness. Here, we will detail how to properly load the patched round ball rifle or the single-shot muzzle-loading pistol.

Round ball shooters can choose between precut patches or loading with bulk patching (right). As the name implies, precut patching is packaged and sold with the patches already cut to the proper diameter. They are available in a variety of thicknesses. Bulk patching is usually nothing more than a strip or square of pillow ticking, or other suitable patching material, that must be trimmed to size during loading. Most round ball shooters today tend to favor precut patches because they are so readily available and do make loading quicker and easier.

Correct lubrication of the patching material is extremely important (below). The first benefit you'll readily notice is that a lubed patch is much easier to get into the bore and push down the barrel with the ramrod. The second benefit is accuracy. Good accuracy with a patched round ball is dependent upon a properly lubed patch.

PATCHING is available precut into circles of the appropriate diameter or in bulk, either in strips or squares.

Patch lubes are as varied as the shooters who load and shoot a patched round ball. Many target shooters rely on nothing more than a saliva-dampened patch. Keep in mind that the target shooter generally loads and fires his rifle within a few minutes. This does not give the saliva time to dry up, dampen the powder charge or cause rust in the bore. If the rifle is being carried for hunting, one of the nondrying, noncorrosive lubes is a much better choice. In the past, shooters sometimes relied on lubes made from bear fat or sperm whale oil. Some of today's shooters often use a homemade patch lube made of cooking shortening and beeswax, or a natural lubricant such as mineral oil. Muzzleloader suppliers now market a wide variety of effective patch lubes that aid loading, reduce friction for better accuracy and prevent the

Types of Patch Lubes

SALIVA serves as a good patch lube provided you plan on firing the gun before the patch has a chance to dry out.

COOKING SHORTENING is an inexpensive lube choice, and it remains soft even in cold temperatures.

powder charge from burning through the cloth patch. Those shooters who rely on precut patches can choose between prelubed (right) or regular, nonlubed patches.

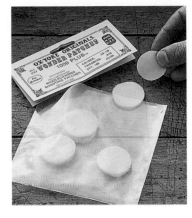

Once the ignition system has been cleared, the barrel wiped clean of oil and the proper powder charge poured through the muzzle, the rifle is ready for loading the patch and ball. If you're using a prelubed, precut patch, center it directly over the bore. Next, place a ball of the proper diameter in the center of the patch. A little thumb pressure pushes the ball and patch slightly into the bore, holding the two in place. Then, using the 4- or 5-inch rod of a ball or short starter, push the patch and ball on into the bore. Finally, use the ramrod to push the patched ball down the bore and on top of the powder charge.

When loading with bulk patching, prepare the rifle in the same manner by clearing the ignition system and bore, followed by pouring in the powder charge. Then, place the strip or square of lubed patching material over the bore; push the ball in slightly with thumb pressure. Next, push the patching and ball below the crown of the muzzle with a ball starter featuring a short 1/4- to 1/2-inch starting rod. Cut the patching flush with the muzzle, using a sharp knife. Push the perfectly patched ball on into the bore with the longer 4- or 5-inch rod of the starter. To finish, use the ramrod to seat the patched ball over the powder charge.

How to Load Using Precut Patches

CENTER a lubed, precut patch over the bore (left). Place a round ball on the patch and press it in place, using slight thumb pressure (right). Push the ball into the bore, using the ball starter; then finish with the ramrod.

How to Load Using Bulk Patches

PUSH a round ball and the lubricated area of bulk patching material below the crown of the muzzle, using a short starting rod (left). Use a knife (right) to cut the patching flush with the muzzle (inset). Finish seating the patched ball over the powder charge with the ball starter and ramrod.

LOADING TIP: Mark the ramrod with a fingernail file (above) or permanent marker after the projectile is properly seated over the powder charge. (Don't weaken the ramrod by scoring it with a knife or other sharp object.) Assuming you don't change loads, you can use the mark to ensure that each projectile is seated to the same depth. The mark can also be used to determine whether a gun is loaded or unloaded.

Loading the Conical Bullet

Conical bullets for muzzleloading rifles fall into two categories – *slip fit* or *interference fit* bullets. Both types require lubrication to obtain good accuracy. Most of the bullet makers currently selling cylindrical bullets for the black powder shooter offer these bullets prelubed. When casting your own or buying nonlubed conical bullets, always generously apply a good commercial bullet lube to the grease grooves of the bullets before loading them (opposite page).

The hollow-base Minie bullet of the Civil War is a great example of a slip fit bullet. This bullet is smaller in diameter than the land-to-land measurement of the rifle or rifled musket bore it is loaded into and fired from. As you might imagine, these bullets literally fall in when inserted into the muzzle. Very little, if any, resistance is felt when the bullet is pushed down the bore with the ramrod. Still, when loading a slip fit bullet, always make sure that the bullet is all the way down on top of the powder before attempting to shoot the frontloader.

It is this poor fit with the bore that causes most of today's muzzleloader gunmakers to recommend not loading and shooting such bullets. However, an occasional maker of big-game hunting rifles and a few suppliers of reproduction Civil War muskets do promote the use of slip fit bullets. One word of caution if you do load and shoot such a loose-fitting bullet: always make sure that the bullet has been seated over the powder charge. Check it occasionally if the rifle is being carried on a hunt. Any bullet that practically falls into the bore can just as easily slide forward if the muzzleloader is carried muzzle down. If the bullet slides forward an inch or so, the result will probably be nothing more than poor accuracy. However, if the bullet slides forward as much as 4 or 5 inches or more, the bullet could act the same as a barrel obstruction and cause the barrel to burst.

Interference fit bullets come in a variety of designs and weights, but all share a common feature: an oversized band or surface that must be engraved by the rifling during loading. Because the bullet has to be forced into the rifling to form the interference fit with the bore, these bullets must be cast or swaged from soft, pure lead.

Most conicals of this design feature a series of bearing bands that either ride directly on the top of the rifling lands, or are engraved by the lands of the rifling. To properly fit with the bore, at least one of these bands must be 1 or 2 thousandths of an inch larger than the land-to-land measurement of the barrel.

The Thompson/Center "Maxi-Ball" is one of the more popular interference fit conical hunting bullets used during modern times. This bullet features three bearing bands. When loaded into the bore, the band at the base of the bullet and another center band are easily slipped into the bore and ride directly on top of the lands. The band situated near the nose of the bullet is several thousandths of an inch oversized and must be forced into the rifling. This is easily done by pushing on the nose of the bullet with a short starter. Once the rifling has cut the soft lead band, the bullet can be pushed down the bore with the ramrod to be seated over the powder charge.

Interference fit bullets stay in place over the powder charge better than slip fit bullets. However, once the rifling has engraved the soft lead band or oversized surface of the bullet, this fit is still loose, at best. With the rifle carried muzzle down, the jar of jumping down off a log, for example, could be enough to cause the bullet to move forward off the powder charge. When hunting with any bore-sized conical bullet, always check several times during the course of a day's hunt to make sure that the bullet is properly seated over the powder charge.

Loading Saboted Bullets

The key to great accuracy with saboted bullets begins with loading the plastic sabot and bullet into a rifle with the correct rate of rifling twist. Rifles that tend to perform best with this projectile system are those that feature rifling grooves that spiral with a fast twist of 1-turn-in-20 to 38 inches.

A proper-diameter bullet and sabot present a relatively snug fit with the rifling of the bore. Because bullet diameters loaded with certain sabots can differ as much as .001 inch or .002 inch, some combinations will load more tightly than others. For instance, sabots for shooting .44-caliber pistol bullets from a .50-caliber muzzleloader will accept bullets of .429- to .431-inch diameters. The smaller diameter will offer less resistance than the larger diameter, but the tighter-fitting bullet could be more accurate.

When loading a saboted bullet, insert the bullet into the cup of the plastic sabot (below). Make sure that the base of the bullet sits flat against the bottom of the cup. Next, insert the combination into the bore of the muzzleloader, slightly starting the saboted bullet with thumb or palm pressure. If it's a really tight-fitting sabot and bullet, you may need to use a bullet short starter to push the combination on into the bore. Quite often, the bullet and sabot can be pushed into the bore with nothing more than palm or thumb pressure.

If you've only pushed the sabot and bullet in flush with the muzzle, grab the ramrod 6 or 7 inches above the bullet and push it on into the bore. Then, slide your hand on up the ramrod and push the bullet and sabot on down the bore to seat solidly over the powder charge. If you've used a bullet starter to push the sabot and bullet into the bore, insert the ramrod and push the combination on down the barrel until it's resting tightly against the powder charge.

Most shooters today rely on the one-piece plastic sabot designs. Lubricants are not used for loading and shooting. The plastic compresses readily and, when loaded into a good bore, the slick plastic sabot is relatively easy to seat with the ramrod. However, because there is no lube to keep powder fouling soft, wiping the bore clean after each shot is crucial to obtaining the best possible accuracy.

How to Load Conical and Saboted Bullets

APPLY lube (if necessary) to conical bullets (top). If you're shooting saboted bullets, place the bullet into the cup of the plasic sabot (bottom).

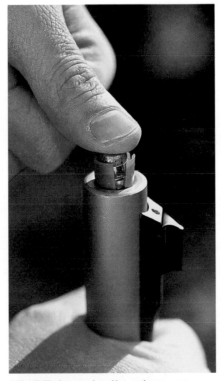

START the projectile, using your thumb (above) or the short rod on a bullet starter.

PUSH the projectile about 6 inches into the bore with the long rod of the bullet starter. Finish seating the projectile with the ramrod (above).

Loading with Shot

Shotguns were never designed to be precision shooting instruments. Muzzleloading scatterguns from the past were developed as a hunter's tool – a firearm that still allowed the hunter to take game with even a haphazardly aimed shot. Instead of a single projectile, shotguns rely on a shot charge that throws hundreds of much smaller projectiles, or pellets, at the game being hunted. The manner in which a particular shotgun and load patterns these pellets determines effectiveness.

Modern breechloading shotguns, and a few of the more recently introduced muzzleloading shotguns, are built with barrels that feature a choke constriction. This tightening of the bore at the muzzle will affect how well the gun patterns (below). Generally speaking, the tighter the constriction, the tighter the pattern. This means that a true cylinder-bore barrel will print a very open, wide pattern.

Muzzleloading shotguns from the past, and the close reproductions of these guns offered today, do not feature a choke of any sort. (Makers didn't truly understand the technique of choking shotgun barrels until the last half of the nineteenth century, after the heyday of original muzzleloading shotguns.) Properly loaded, however, these open-choked front-loading smoothbores are capable of throwing some very effective game-taking patterns. The secret lies in how the scattergun is loaded.

The sequence of wads stuffed in through the muzzle plays an instrumental role in obtaining nice, even

Cutaway view of a loaded black powder shotgun

patterns at game-taking ranges. Most experienced muzzleloading shotgunners wipe the bore of the smoothbore clean of oil and then snap several caps on a percussion gun to clear it of oil. If the shotgun is a flintlock, they make sure the vent hole is cleared.

Once the gun is readied, the powder charge is dumped in through the muzzle. Over the powder charge goes a heavy over-powder card of about .125-inch thickness. Directly over this, the shooter ramrods down a cushion wad that's usually about ½ inch in thickness. These wads are often punched from a fibrous material, such as a common construction board known as Celotex®, or something similar. Many shooters soak the cushion wad in cooking oil so it loads easier.

How Choke Affects the Shot Pattern

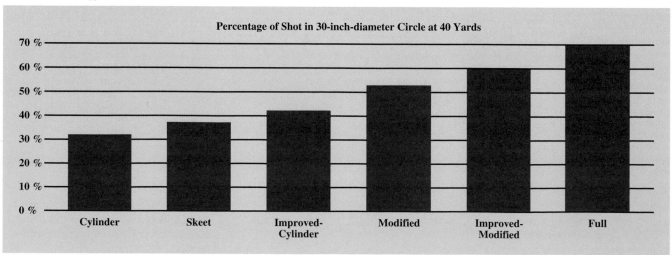

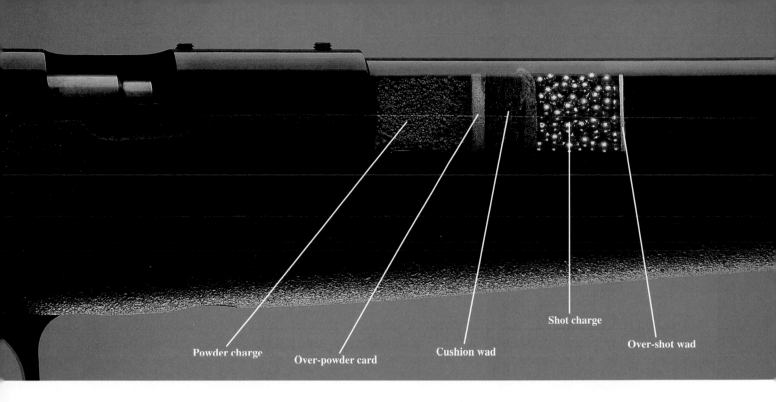

Powder charge
Over-powder card
Cushion wad
Shot charge
Over-shot wad

Directly over the cushion wad goes the shot charge, followed by a thin over-shot wad that keeps the pellets from rolling back out when the shotgun is carried muzzle down. Don't use the same heavy wad material used as an over-powder card. Anything this heavy can and will affect the center density, resulting in a pattern that resembles a donut, with most of the shot around the edges and little toward the center. A thin, .030-inch over-shot wad is the most widely used, but more and more shooters are turning to even lighter over-shot wads made from cork or Styrofoam®.

Experienced shooters often experiment slightly with the exact combination (and thicknesses) of wads to achieve the best pattern. No two shotguns shoot exactly the same, so take the time to pattern your gun before you go hunting.

When loading a muzzle-loading shotgun with a choked barrel, you'll find it difficult to force the thick cushion wad through the constriction. One remedy is to use the ¼-inch-thick felt wads offered by several muzzleloading suppliers (right). These are flexible enough to be pushed through the constriction, one at a time, to build a ½- to ¾-inch cushion wad on top of the over-powder card.

If your shotgun is equipped with one of the screw-in chokes, you may want to remove the choke when loading the shotgun, especially if the choke is one of the "extra-full" turkey hunting chokes. Muzzleloading shotguns that have a screw-in choke tend to perform well when loaded with one of the one-piece, plastic wads used for loading modern shotshells (right). This replaces both the over-powder card and cushion wad. However, the choke definitely has to be removed in order to get one of these plastic wads through the muzzle.

When loading either an open-choked frontloading smoothbore or one of the more modern choked muzzleloading shotguns, try to load with nearly equal volumes of powder and shot. Experienced muzzleloading shotgun shooters have long realized that when one is loaded way out of proportion to the other, patterns suffer.

Also, the coarser grades of powder have consistently produced some of the best patterns. Always load with either FFg black powder or Pyrodex "RS" powders. The amount of powder and shot loaded will vary according to the intended target – an afternoon of claybirding or going after an ol' tom turkey require different loads.

Loading the Percussion Revolver

Practically all of the reproduction cap and ball revolvers sold in the U.S. originate in either Italy or Spain. To keep the guns from rusting during the long voyage, the manufacturers commonly douse these guns with lubricant. Before these guns can be loaded and fired, they must be disassembled and cleaned thoroughly. Importers usually include directions for breaking the guns down for cleaning. If instructions aren't included, the designs are so simple that anyone can normally figure out how to remove the cylinder from the barrel and receiver in order to clean them free of the heavy oil.

Percussion wheelguns are typically of two common designs dating from the past: the open-topped Colt or the closed-frame Remington. Even though the two designs vary slightly in appearance and how they are taken down for cleaning (p. 99), they are basically loaded the same.

To prepare a percussion wheelgun for loading, first place the hammer in the half-cock position. This will allow the cylinder to rotate freely. Now, place a percussion cap on each of the five or six nipples. Then, cock the hammer back and snap a cap on each chamber to blow or burn any oil out of the nipples. The percussion revolver is now ready to be loaded.

Place the hammer back on half cock so the cylinder rotates freely. Measure out the proper powder charge and pour it into a chamber. Next, place a ball over the mouth of that chamber. Ideally, the ball should be several thousandths of an inch larger than the chamber itself and should not drop down into the chamber. To push the oversized ball into the chamber, rotate the cylinder until the ball aligns with the loading lever attached to the bottom of the barrel and frame of the revolver. Using the lever, force the ball into the chamber. If the ball is the correct diameter, a thin ring of lead should peel off as the ball is being pushed into the chamber. Repeat the process until all of the chambers are loaded.

The tight fit is necessary to prevent the ball from working forward during recoil and keeping the cylinder from rotating around to align with the barrel. Even so, the fit isn't tight enough to guarantee that fire from one chamber won't find its way around the ball in another chamber, causing that chamber to fire simultaneously. This condition is known as a *chain fire,* which can be damaging to both the revolver and the shooter's nerves. To prevent a chain fire, always dab a small amount of muzzleloading lube over the top of each loaded chamber. Another method is to place a felt wad between the ball and powder charge.

Finally, place a percussion cap on each of the nipples, and you're ready to do some shooting. The chambers of even the largest percussion revolvers offer very limited room for powder, so stick with the finer granulations. Most revolver manufacturers and importers recommend loading and shooting either FFFg black powder or Pyrodex "P" grade powders. Also, if you plan to carry the loaded revolver in a holster, safety dictates that you keep the hammer down on an uncapped chamber.

Whether it's a muzzleloading rifle, musket, shotgun or handgun, always practice good judgment when loading and shooting a frontloading gun. Consistency has its rewards, and when you are loading a muzzleloader, it enhances accuracy and performance. Treat every load as a custom reload and you're sure to be a lot happier with the results.

How to Load Percussion Revolvers

PLACE a percussion cap on each of the revolver's nipples. The cylinder will rotate freely if the hammer is in the half-cock position.

SNAP the caps on each chamber by moving the hammer back to the full-cock position and pulling the trigger. This ensures that each nipple is clear.

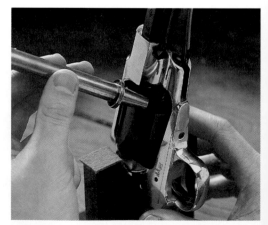

POUR a measured powder charge into a single chamber. A loading stand is a handy tool for steadying the revolver.

76

Black Powder Loading Tips

Getting your frontloader to hit where you're aiming, shot after shot, begins with good loading practices. Here are a few tips that will help to ensure that you achieve optimal accuracy and performance.

• Always buy the best-quality muzzleloader you can afford. A $200 muzzleloader will not have the same-quality barrel that you'll find on a $400 muzzleloader. So don't expect it to shoot as accurately.

• Be absolutely sure that you are buying the right diameter projectiles for the gun you own.

• No matter which projectile you purchase, be sure that it is compatible with your gun's rate of rifling twist.

• Always use your ramrod and cleaning jag with a dry patch to wipe the bore of your rifle clean of oil before pouring in a powder charge.

• Rely on a quality measure to determine your powder charge. Also, always use the same powder measure, because there can be as much as a 10 to 15 percent variance in charges from measure to measure.

• If the patched round ball, conical, or saboted bullet you are loading fits so tightly that it is deformed by the time it's forced into the muzzle with a starter, it's not likely to shoot accurately. Try a different combination.

• Seat the projectile with the ramrod in one continuous stroke. Trying to ram the projectile down the bore with short jabs only deforms the ball or bullet and increases the chances of getting the projectile stuck in the bore before it's properly seated.

• Never bounce the ramrod on the seated projectile, or pound on a seated projectile with the ramrod in an effort to secure it firmly over the powder charge. This only results in damage to the ball or bullet and destroys accuracy.

Point the gun's muzzle away from you at all times

• Carefully study the owner's manual and other instructional materials that came with your gun. Use the manufacturer's recommended powder granulations and charges. Never exceed recommended maximum limits.

• Muzzleloading single-shot pistols are loaded in the same manner as a rifle. With one of the short-barreled handguns, use the same techniques and guidelines for loading a muzzleloading rifle. Remember, the barrel is much shorter, so take extra precautions to keep the muzzle angled away from your face and body (above).

PLACE a round ball over the mouth of the chamber. Only a ball that is too small in diameter will drop down into the chamber.

PUSH the ball into the chamber with the loading lever. Repeat the process until each chamber is loaded.

DAB a small amount of muzzleloader lube over each loaded chamber to prevent a chain fire. Place caps on the nipples to shoot the gun.

Shooting Muzzleloaders

Getting the most out of any muzzleloader requires that the shooter give his fullest attention to the effort. Different types of muzzleloaders require slightly different loading and shooting techniques, and some may produce better accuracy when fired from a particular shooting position. The following describes what it takes to get the best performance from each of the different frontloading designs.

Shooting Flintlocks

Hunting with a flintlock offers the ultimate challenge for today's black powder burner. Modern copies of early rifles, handguns, Revolutionary War muskets and shotguns await the shooter who wants to test his or her abilites with flint-and-steel ignition frontloaders.

Before loading and attempting to shoot a flintlock, first inspect the size of the flint. With the hammer at half cock and the frizzen down, the flint should almost meet the frizzen (below). If it doesn't, replace the flint with one of the correct size.

When loading a flintlock, begin by making sure the frizzen is flipped forward, in the open position. Then, lower the hammer so the sharpened edge of the flint is facing downward into the empty priming pan. With the hammer and frizzen in these positions, there is no chance of the hammer accidentally falling, striking the frizzen and causing the muzzleloader to fire as it is being loaded.

Experienced shooters always wipe the bore free of oil before pouring in a measured powder charge, to eliminate ignition problems. Once the gun is loaded (p. 70), the lock is ready to be primed.

Draw the hammer back to half cock. This positions the hammer far enough back to enable you to clear the vent hole with a paper clip or vent pick. Next, trickle a few grains of dustlike priming powder,

How to Shoot Flintlocks

CHECK that the flint almost meets the frizzen with the hammer at half cock.

MOVE the frizzen forward to expose the flintlock's pan.

LOWER the hammer toward the pan, and load the powder and projectile.

CLEAR the vent hole with a paper clip (above) or a vent pick.

TRICKLE priming powder into the pan and then lower the frizzen.

PULL the hammer back to full cock, and the gun is ready to fire.

Hunter shooting a flintlock

normally FFFFg black powder, into the flash pan. Then, flip the frizzen rearward to cover the pan.

To fire the gun, draw the hammer backward to full cock. As you pull the trigger, the hammer falls forward and the flint hits the frizzen. The force results in sparks, which fall into the exposed powder in the pan. A very small amount of the resulting flash enters the vent hole in the side of the barrel and reaches the main powder charge. If you've done everything correctly, ignition occurs and the muzzleloader belches out a billowing cloud of white smoke.

Experienced flintlock shooters have adopted some tips and tricks to make their guns more reliable. At the bottom of this page are a handful of the best of these tips. But keep in mind that even the best shooters can't make these arms 100 percent surefire!

Tips for Improving Flintlock Ignition

REMOVE small flint chips by tapping the flint with the back side of a knife. This keeps the flint sharp.

WRAP the flint with a piece of leather so the jaw of the hammer can grip the smooth flint securely.

FILL the priming pan about half full. Overfilling the pan usually leads to slow ignition.

TILT the gun slightly and tap it to move the priming powder in the pan away from the vent hole.

Shooting Percussion Caplocks

PLACE a percussion cap on the nipple after loading the powder and projectile. The hammer should be in the half-cock position.

PULL the hammer back to full cock. The gun is now ready to be fired.

REMOVE the cap after the shot. Use a decapper tool, if necessary.

Before attempting to load and fire a percussion caplock, take a few minutes to ensure that the bore and ignition system are free of oil or solvents left from a previous cleaning. First, run a few dry patches down the bore, using the ramrod with a cleaning jag threaded into one end. Next, snap two or three caps on the nipple, or each nipple if the gun has multiple barrels or chambers. This blows or burns any oil left in the flash channel through the nipple and into the barrel. Most misfires with percussion guns are the result of oil or solvent in the ignition system.

Before loading a side-hammer percussion caplock, place the hammer in the half-cock position. Next, measure out a powder charge and pour the powder into the muzzle. Experienced shooters often tap the side of the barrel with a few brisk taps, or thump the heel of the butt-plate against the ground, to make sure that at least a few of the powder granules find their way into the flash channel and closer to the base of the nipple. This ensures better ignition.

Once the powder has been poured into the barrel, start the ball or bullet of your choice into the barrel and, using the ramrod, seat the projectile over the powder charge. Make sure that the projectile is firmly seated over the powder, but don't pound on it with the ramrod.

Place a percussion cap on the nipple, making sure that it is firmly seated. To fire the gun, pull the hammer back to full cock, take aim at your target and pull the trigger. As the hammer falls, it ignites the priming charge inside the percussion cap, and the resulting flash travels through the flash channel inside the nipple and into the barrel. Provided you have properly loaded the muzzleloader, ignition should be fairly instant.

Shooting In-Line Percussion Caplocks

The number one apprehension of the black powder shooter is whether or not his frontloader will fire when the trigger is pulled. After all, improved ignition is what drove muzzleloader development through the ages. Shooters have long recognized that the more instantaneous the ignition, the better the chances of hitting the target with accuracy. The in-line percussion ignition system answers these concerns.

To shoot an in-line muzzleloader, begin by running a dry patch down the bore and snapping a few caps to clear the flash channel. After loading the projectile, pull the hammer back to cock the gun. Next, place a percussion cap on the nipple. The gun is ready to be fired after you move the safety to the "off" position.

One of the greatest advantages of the modern in-line percussion muzzleloader is that nearly all are built with a modern safety system, similar to those found on center-fire rifles. This allows the shooter, especially the hunter, to pack one of these frontloaders with the hammer already at full cock. Once the game being hunted has been spotted, the hunter simply reaches up and slips off the safety, takes aim and fires.

Some of the finest in-line muzzleloader designs also incorporate a secondary safety which forms a true hammer block when engaged. On the Knight Rifles in-line muzzleloaders this safety is in the form of a knurled ring situated at the rear of the plunger-style hammer. When this ring is threaded forward it will prevent the hammer from falling forward far enough to strike the capped nipple. Even if the rifle is dropped from a tree stand 20 feet above the ground, this rifle cannot fire when the secondary safety is engaged.

PULL the hammer back to cock the muzzleloader after it has been loaded. The safety should be in the "on" position.

PLACE a percussion cap on the nipple.

MOVE the safety to the "off" position when you are ready to shoot.

OFFHAND. Stand sideways to the target with legs spread to shoulder width. Keep your left elbow close to your body. If your gun has a sling, wrap your left arm in it for added support.

Shooting Positions

The finest muzzleloading rifle that's been loaded with an optimal combination of powder and projectile is still only as accurate as the shooter firing the rifle. If you have spent a significant amount of money to buy the very best quality muzzleloader available, and have taken the time and effort to properly match the frontloader with the right powder charge and saboted bullet, conical or patched round ball, you should expect to be rewarded with good accuracy. That is, provided you have also taken the time to develop your shooting postures.

Generally speaking, muzzleloading riflemen master five positions in order to be prepared for every shooting and hunting situation. The positions are: standing (offhand), sitting, kneeling, prone, and shooting from a solid rest. The accompanying photos show the correct positions for a right-hand shooter.

The very design of certain muzzleloading rifles makes them nearly impossible to fire from some shooting

SITTING. Bring your knees up toward your chest and place both elbows on your knees, avoiding bone-to-bone contact.

KNEELING. Sit on your right foot and put your left foot forward. Rest your left elbow on the knee.

PRONE. With your left elbow just left of the gun, pull your right leg forward to lift your stomach, so your breathing doesn't affect the shot.

SOLID REST. Use fallen trees or other objects to help steady your aim. Don't place the gun's forearm on the rest because the gun will bounce from the recoil.

positions. For example, the long and graceful Kentucky or Pennsylvania rifles were never intended to be fired from the prone position.

These are offhand rifles, most commonly featuring a considerable amount of drop in the comb of the buttstock and a very pronounced crescent-shaped buttplate (above). The sharply curved brass or steel buttplate can cause quite a bit of discomfort when one of these rifles is fired with the butt held squarely against the shoulder. Correctly positioned, the curved buttplate should follow the contour of the upper bicep, placing the toe of the buttplate practically into the armpit.

When pulled in tightly against the upper portion of the arm muscle, an authentically styled American longrifle produces very tolerable recoil. However, when a rifle of this type is fired from any position that requires the butt to be placed flat against the shoulder, be ready for a little pain, especially if you happen to be shooting a healthy hunting load.

The recoil generated by a muzzleloader is noticeably different from that produced by a modern centerfire rifle. Keep in mind that the fast-burning, smokeless powder fired in a centerfire rifle cartridge is commonly consumed in only about 12 to 14 inches of barrel. To the shooter, this translates into recoil that's normally not much more than a sharp rearward jolt against the shoulder. The rifle itself exhibits very little rearward travel.

When you fire a heavy 90- or 100-grain hunting charge of black powder or Pyrodex out of a big-bore muzzleloading hunting rifle, it can take 20 or more inches of barrel to fully burn the entire powder charge. The recoil produced by a muzzleloader is a much longer push. Combined with the resistance of a heavy lead conical bullet (which could weigh 400 to 500 grains), the slow-burning muzzleloading propellants produce recoil that can pound a shooter backward. When fired from the offhand, kneeling or sitting positions, this recoil more often than not just rocks the shooter backward. However, if such loads are fired from the prone position, where the body cannot rock with the recoil, be prepared for a real beating.

If you plan to compete in black powder target competitions, practice your offhand skills. Most of the muzzleloading competitions held around the country consist of offhand matches at 25, 50, and 100 yards.

While the muzzleloading hunter should be skilled enough to pull off an accurate offhand shot, the experienced hunter always tries to shoot from a more solid position. The kneeling and sitting positions offer most shooters a much steadier shot. And, if you happen to be hunting with saboted bullets and one of the modern in line percussion rifles equipped with a good rubber recoil pad, the recoil is still tame enough to warrant shooting from the prone position.

Nothing takes the place of a good rest. Wilderness travelers of the 1700s and 1800s found powder and lead to be scarce outside civilization. For that reason, it's a good bet that few chanced a wasted shot by throwing their rifle to the shoulder and taking an offhand shot if a good rest was close at hand. A leaning rest against a tree is much steadier than a freestanding shot, and a downed log or rock can offer the sitting or kneeling shooter an even steadier rest.

Many early westward adventurers carried a rest right along with them in the form of crossed sticks. As the name implies, two sticks or poles of about 3 feet in length were loosely tied or attached together.

The arrangement could be spread to form an "X"-shaped rest for the forestock of a rifle. Modern crossed sticks (above), like those of the past, are just tall enough to provide a sturdy rest for shooting from a sitting position.

When working up loads (p. 89) or sighting in (p. 84), do all of your shooting from a good solid bench rest. The steadier the rifle during shooting, the more consistently you'll group your shots. Occasionally, you may find that a particular rifle or load tends to shoot slightly higher when fired from the bench rather than one of the freehand positions. Because the forearm of the rifle just sits on the shooting bags when fired, recoil from slow-burning powder and a heavy projectile can cause the muzzle to jump ever so slightly before the bullet leaves the muzzle. This causes impact above the point of aim on the target.

Once you have the muzzleloader grouping satisfactorily at the distance you intend to shoot, try a few shots without the sandbags or shooting rest. Grasp the forearm of the rifle and let your elbow rest on the shooting bench. Even though the groups fired probably won't be as tight as those fired from a sandbag rest, you'll get a better idea of your true point of impact downrange.

Sights & Scopes

Veteran black powder shooters with years of experience using a variety of muzzleloaders will tell you that a muzzleloading rifle is only as good as its barrel. True enough. They will also tell you that it takes a good set of iron sights or a high-quality scope on that barrel before you can effectively harness any of the inherent accuracy that a frontloading rifle possesses. If the muzzleloader you're shooting is fitted with a poor sighting system, it's doubtful that you'll ever achieve acceptable accuracy, no matter how high the quality of the barrel or your eyesight.

Open Sights

Many reproduction muzzleloaders sold during the 1960s and 1970s (still used today) were built with fixed, nonadjustable rear sights (opposite page). Sights of this type were a common feature on original muzzleloading guns of centuries past, but they have found little favor among the majority of 1990s shooters. Because of that, the bulk of frontloading rifles currently manufactured come fitted with a rear sight that's fully adjustable for windage (left/right) and elevation (up/down). Sighting has become a much easier chore. There are, however, a few muzzleloaders on the modern market that specifically feature only a fixed rear sight. In most cases,

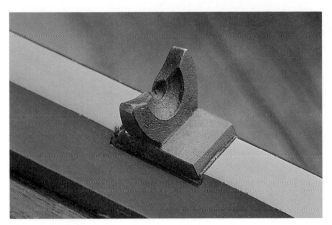

Fixed rear sight

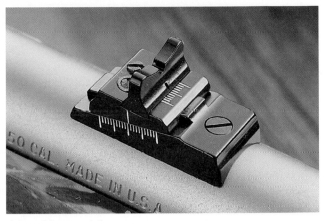

Adjustable rear sight

the decision of the manufacturer to use sights of this type was based on maintaining the muzzleloader's authentic design, not keeping the price down.

So-called "fixed" sights are still adjustable, but require the shooter to do a little filing for elevation or tapping of the sights in one direction or another to change how the shots impact on the target. Rear sights of this type commonly feature a base with a pronounced bevel on the front and rear edges. These fit tightly into a dovetailed slot that has been milled into the top of the barrel. To adjust a fixed rear sight for windage requires that the sight be tapped slightly in one direction or the other. If the front sight is also attached to the barrel using a dovetailed slot, it can be adjusted in the same way.

When adjusting fixed sights for windage, the rear sight is moved in the direction you want the shot to move. The front sight, however, must be moved in the opposite direction of the desired point of impact. If the rifle shoots considerably to one side, you may want to make slight adjustments on both the rear and front sights instead of trying to make the complete adjustment by moving one or the other. In extreme cases of windage adjustment, this method will prevent a rear or front sight from practically falling out of the slot in the barrel. Once the adjustments have been made, you may also need to use a hammer and steel punch to tap down the edges of the slots to keep the sights from slipping out due to a loose fit.

Elevation adjustments with fixed sights generally call for some file work. To bring up the point of impact, the top of the front sight blade must be filed down. If the rifle shoots high, the notch in the rear sight can be filed deeper to bring down the point of impact.

A number of muzzleloading suppliers offer replacement sights. However, if you're considering replacing a fixed rear sight with a higher or lower sight in your attempts to adjust for elevation, it is worth checking out sights that are fully adjustable. If you

ever change loads with the rifle you could find yourself having to make sight alterations. Built-in adjustments make the task much less time-consuming.

The adjustable rear sights (above) found on most of today's rifles make fine-tuning shot placement much quicker and easier. Again, remember to move the rear sight in the direction you want the shot to go: left, right, up or down.

Here are a few points to be aware of when you evaluate sights. Just because the set of sights found on a rifle are fixed, don't write them off as being of lower quality. Many of the highest-quality custom rifles now being built feature a nonadjustable rear sight in order to authentically copy a rifle design from the past. Numerous record-setting competition shooters rely totally on nonadjustable rear sights. Conversely, just because the sights installed on a rifle are of the adjustable type doesn't make them superior to all nonadjustable sights.

The design of the sights on the barrel can enhance (or detract from) the overall aesthetics of muzzleloading rifles. The quality of the sights cannot be judged by their appearance alone; they may look good but render poor sighting, or seem ill-suited but give excellent visual aid. Sights play such a vital role in obtaining good accuracy with any muzzleloading rifle that your evaluation should be based on factors more important than appearance.

For example, lower-priced good-looking reproduction guns too often come with a front sight that's so thick and heavy that it completely hides the bullseye of a target or covers the chest cavity of a white-tailed deer at 100 yards. Many of these guns also have an adjustable rear sight that cannot withstand the jar of stiff recoil, or, in some cases, even changes in the weather. In other words, all the meticulous settings made by the shooter do not hold fast as expected. Such sights will never reward you with the accuracy you deserve and should demand.

Scopes

Installation of telescopic sights aboard muzzleloading big-game rifles has become commonplace as a result of legalization over the past quarter century. During the 1970s, when many of the muzzleloader-only big-game seasons were first established, scopes were allowed in only about a half dozen states. Today, more than half of the states permit the muzzleloading hunter to use optical scopes with varying degrees of magnification limits.

Mounting scopes on muzzleloading rifles has been a controversial subject for years. On one side of the argument are devoted shooters and hunters of traditionally styled muzzleloading guns who believe that a scope has absolutely no business on a frontloading rifle. On the other side are dedicated big-game hunters who have seriously educated and equipped themselves

for muzzleloading solely to expand their hunting seasons and specific game-taking opportunities. They want a scope on their hunting rifle – whether it is a modern centerfire gun or one that loads from the front.

Obviously, a quality scope offers the big-game muzzleloading hunter a distinct advantage over fixed and adjustable sights: it provides the shooter with the possibility of immediate pinpoint, crosshair alignment on the vital, clean-kill section of a distant target when the shot is fired. Also, shooters who are visually impaired will find it much easier to cope with a scope than open sights. A crisp, clear scope with some magnification allows a shooter to better identify his target before squeezing off the shot.

When selecting a scope for a muzzleloading rifle, keep in mind that the recoil from the slow-burning black powder loads results in more rearward travel of the gun than the recoil produced by the smokeless powder loads in a modern centerfire. Consider only those scopes that offer a minimum of 3 inches of eye relief (opposite page); if you can find a model that has 4 inches, you'll be that much better off. Be sure to utilize every fraction of an inch of that eye relief: get too close to the rear lens objective of a scope on a

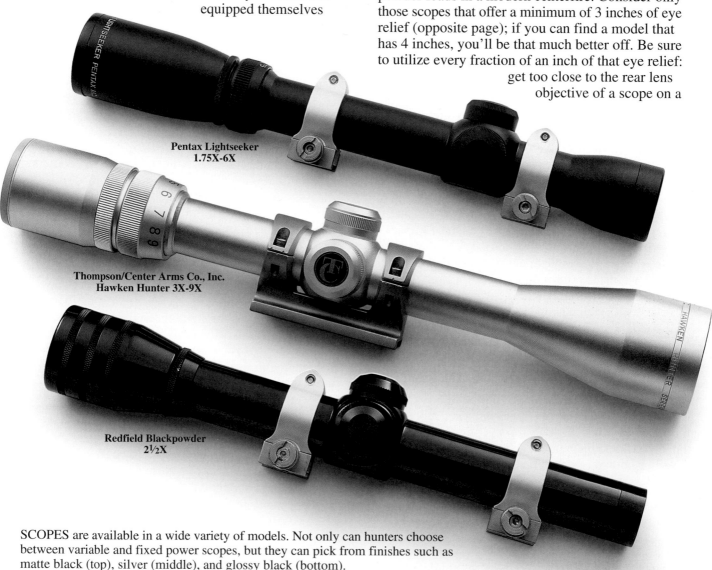

**Pentax Lightseeker
1.75X-6X**

**Thompson/Center Arms Co., Inc.
Hawken Hunter 3X-9X**

**Redfield Blackpowder
2½X**

SCOPES are available in a wide variety of models. Not only can hunters choose between variable and fixed power scopes, but they can pick from finishes such as matte black (top), silver (middle), and glossy black (bottom).

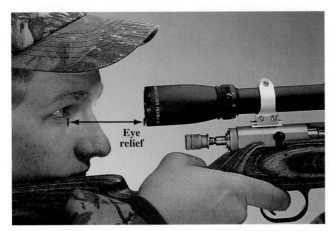

EYE RELIEF for a muzzleloader scope should measure at least 3 inches.

muzzleloader (especially when shooting heavy hunting loads), and the recoil could push the rifle back far enough to leave a nasty cut above your eye.

A few states impose a maximum magnification regulation for scopes used during the muzzleloading seasons. Before installing a scope, make sure it is legal where you plan to hunt. In states where shooters have the freedom to use any power scope, the degree of magnification is a personal thing. Most whitetails are shot at distances well inside 75 yards, so a good 4X scope is normally sufficient. However, whitetails in the Midwest and other big game in the West are often taken at ranges exceeding 100 yards. A quality 2X-7X or 3X-9X variable power scope can make one of the modern in-line percussion rifles a more versatile hunting rifle. When you are faced with close-range shots between 25 and 75 yards, a lower power setting is readily available, making it easier to spot game in the scope. For those shots from 100 to 150 yards, a higher magnification setting is at your fingertips.

SCOPE PROTECTORS shield scopes from the corrosive black powder residue and percussion cap particles thrown by in-line muzzleloaders. Repeated shooting without a scope protector can mar the scope's finish (inset).

Peep sight

Alternative Sighting Systems

A good peep sight is an excellent alternative to a scope – especially in states where scopes are illegal. Peep sights, sometimes called *receiver* or *aperture* sights, rely on a tiny sighting hole through the center of a small disc instead of the typical "U" or "V" notch generally associated with a rear sight. Such an arrangement provides a more precise sighting system, which many shooters actually prefer over a scope for longer-range target and hunting use.

A number of manufacturers offer peep sights that install easily on some of their rifle models. In the hands of a good shooter, an accurate muzzleloading rifle fitted with a precision peep sight can be deadly on game. Manufacturers recognize that today's hunter wants choices when it comes to the sighting system he or she relies on in the field. Many of the newer models come with receivers or barrels drilled and tapped to accept a wide range of scope bases and rings, as well as peep sights.

As muzzleloading continues to mature into a true hunting sport, regulations are quickly changing to reflect the desires of the hunter. The limitations of early muzzleloading seasons dictated the use of open sights only; now modern scoped muzzleloading hunting rifles are permitted.

The overall benefit of the relaxation in regulations is that they provide a range of hunting options: you can choose to tackle the extreme challenge of hunting with a traditional rifle with open sights, or you can opt to hunt with scopes or peep sights. Today's big-game resources are plentiful and healthy. The more liberally regulated muzzleloading seasons we now enjoy make room out there for everyone.

Developing Effective Loads

There are a number of factors that can and will affect the accuracy of a muzzleloading rifle. Some shooters never end their search for the perfect combination of powder and projectile. Others often take the easy route and simply drop in a recommended powder charge and ramrod whatever projectile they have available down over the powder. It's doubtful that the latter shooters will ever be truly satisfied with the performance of their muzzleloader. The shooter who spends hours at the shooting bench refining, or "tweaking," the load for his or her frontloader, however, will develop the confidence to become very proficient with the rifle.

Powder Charges

Developing effective loads, often called "working up a load," for any rifle begins with selecting the right granulation of black powder or Pyrodex. (See chapter 5, "Powders," for a discussion of the different grades of powders available and the recommended powders for the variety of calibers and types of frontloading guns.) Occasionally, you may discover that a particular gun will perform better with black powder than Pyrodex, or vice versa. When working up a load for a brand-new gun, it's to your benefit to try both types of powder to ensure that you are indeed getting the best accuracy possible.

Before ever loading and shooting a new muzzleloader, take the time to read the manual and any other instructional materials that may have been included. Most manufacturers have already determined the range of powder charges (right) that perform best with their product and will normally provide some loading data as well. While obtaining top accuracy may require that you do some experimenting with the amount of powder loaded, never exceed the manufacturer's recommended maximum powder charges. Loading too little powder rarely results in injury to the shooter, but too much powder can produce dangerous pressures inside the barrel.

Safe and effective experimenting could turn out something like this: if the manufacturer recommends powder charges of 70 to 100 grains of a given powder for a particular projectile, you might find that to get the most out of your muzzleloader requires that you load exactly 85 grains for each and every shot instead of 80 grains. In a particular rifle, a 5-grain-heavier-or-lighter charge can really improve accuracy. So don't be afraid to do a little experimenting.

In many muzzleloading rifles, however, a 5-, 10-, or even 15-grain change in the powder charge being shot won't readily affect how a rifle will group downrange, provided that you load exactly the same charge for each and every shot. Just be sure to stay within the rifle manufacturer's recommended range of powder charges. For the most part, the amount of powder you load simply propels the real shooting star of your load – the projectile.

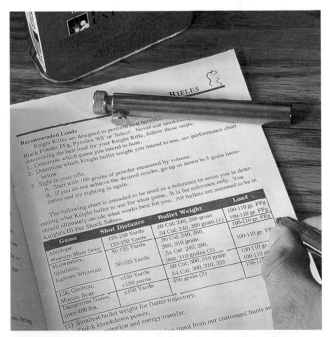

CHECK the owner's manual for your muzzleloader to find the recommended range of powder charges.

Projectiles

If you are loading and shooting either the patched round ball or one of the bore-sized conical bullets, it's important that these be either cast or swaged from soft, pure lead. Even if as little as 2 or 3 percent antimony, tin or other hardeners has been added to the lead, the projectiles will be too hard to produce good accuracy with any muzzleloading rifle. A round ball that has been cast from hard lead cannot be properly gripped by the weave of the patch, ruining accuracy. Conical bullets made of anything but pure lead will resist being engraved by the rifling during loading, making it next to impossible to start them into the muzzle.

Commercially available round balls and conical bullets packaged by a reputable maker will ensure that you're shooting a soft, pure-lead projectile. However, you are likely to encounter cast projectiles on dealers' shelves of dubious origins or you may even be lured into casting your own to help cut the cost of shooting. One way to guarantee that these are soft enough to produce good accuracy from your rifle is to check the lead with your thumbnail. If you can scratch or indent the surface with mere thumb pressure (above), the lead is adequately soft to produce the accuracy you're looking for.

Very slight differences in ball or bullet diameter can also affect accuracy. Be sure that you are loading with the proper-diameter projectiles. If they load way too tightly or practically fall into the bore when started into the muzzle, chances are you're not shooting the right-diameter projectile for your rifle.

Loading with the proper-diameter bullet is critical when firing the modern, saboted bullets. Sabots are commonly color-coded to easily identify the right sabots for a given caliber. However, with several calibers, you'll find that you have a range of sabot choices. For instance, for the .50-caliber rifles, shooters can choose between sabots for shooting .44- or 45-caliber bullets. If a sabot intended for a .45-caliber bullet is loaded with a .44-caliber bullet, the combination will load without any resistance whatsoever. Accuracy will be poor at best. On the other hand, if you try to load a .45-caliber bullet using a sabot sized to load a .44-caliber bullet, it's doubtful that you'll even get the two stuffed through the muzzle. If you do, the combination will load so tightly that either the bullet or the sabot will be damaged by the time it's seated over the powder charge. Again, accuracy will suffer.

In short, it's very important that you have the proper loading components before ever attempting to load and shoot a new muzzleloading rifle. If you plan to shoot target competition and hunt with the same rifle, you may find that you need to work up two different loads. Often, the most accurate loads simply do not generate enough energy to warrant use on big game. Or, in some rifles, you may find that for target competition you must shoot a patched round ball and for hunting you may want to shoot a harder-hitting conical.

Therein lies a problem. Not many rifles will shoot both types of projectiles accurately. This is especially true with rifles designed primarily for shooting a patched round ball. While the slow 1-turn-in-60-to-72-inches rate of twist of the rifling found in these rifles will produce the absolute best accuracy with a patched round ball, they just don't impart enough spin on an elongated, conical bullet to stabilize the projectile in flight.

Those rifles built with a much faster 1-turn-in-20-to-32-inches rate of twist are more likely to produce good target accuracy with a round ball, while also providing optimal accuracy and knockdown power with a conical or saboted bullet. When loading and shooting a patched ball in one of these rifles, a shooter will generally find that the projectile has to be loaded with lighter 40- to 50-grain charges of powder to obtain acceptable accuracy. The lighter charges keep velocities slow enough to allow the patch and ball to be properly spun by the rifling. When loaded with a hefty 90- to 100-grain charge of powder, the fast-twist rifling frequently spins the patch too rapidly to allow it to properly grip the soft lead ball.

When working up loads for hunting big game, you are faced with achieving two goals – to settle on a good accurate load, and to develop a load that produces enough energy to cleanly drop the game being hunted. For big-game hunting, the patched round ball projectile is easily the worst choice. Being a perfect sphere, a ball sheds velocity and energy quickly downrange. A .50-caliber rifle, loaded with 100 grains of FFg black powder or Pyrodex "RS/Select" and a 178-grain patched .490-inch round ball, pushes the projectile from the muzzle at around 1,800 f.p.s. (24- to 28-inch barrel). The load develops right at 1,300 foot-pounds of energy. By the time the ball reaches 100 yards, it is good for only about 400 foot-pounds of energy, not enough to ensure a good clean kill on deer-sized game, let alone something as big as an elk.

Ballistic Loading Chart

SABOTED BULLETS

Bullet/Rifle Description	Range (Yards)	Impact (Inches)	Velocity (ft./sec.)	Energy (ft./lbs.)	Bullet/Rifle Description	Range (Yards)	Impact (Inches)	Velocity (ft./sec.)	Energy (ft./lbs.)
Knight 240-gr. Jacketed/ .50- & .54-cal. Rifles	0	-	1553	1285	Barnes 300-gr. Red Hot Bullet Copper/ .50-cal. Rifle	0	-	1621	1750
	50	1.59	1488	1159		50	2.01	1478	1455
	100	0	1366	995		100	0	1349	1212
	150	-6.21	1260	846		150	-6.60	1237	1020
Barnes 250-gr. Red Hot Bullet Copper/ .50-cal. Rifle	0	-	1682	1570	Knight 310-gr. Lead/ .50- & .54-cal. Rifles	0	-	1447	1441
	50	1.91	1520	1282		50	1.85	1394	1338
	100	0	1374	1047		100	0	1297	1158
	150	-6.33	1248	864		150	-6.99	1212	1011
Knight 260-gr. Jacketed & Lead/ .50- & 54-cal. Rifles	0	-	1524	1340	Knight 325-gr. Jacketed/ .54-cal. Rifle	0	-	1438	1751
	50	1.65	1461	1233		50	1.97	1361	1336
	100	0	1346	1045		100	0	1200	1039
	150	-6.44	1244	894		150	-7.84	1083	846
Knight 300-gr. Jacketed/ .50- & .54-cal. Rifles	0	-	1484	1466	Barnes 325-gr. Red Hot Bullet Copper/ .54-cal. Rifle	0	-	1498	1619
	50	1.74	1431	1364		50	2.26	1369	1353
	100	0	1333	1183		100	0	1257	1140
	150	-6.63	1246	1034		150	-7.83	1163	976

ROUND BALLS

Bullet/Rifle Description	Range (Yards)	Impact (Inches)	Velocity (ft./sec.)	Energy (ft./lbs.)
180-gr. Lead/ .50-cal. Rifle (90-gr. FFg)	0	-	1755	1231
	50	2.36	1231	606
	100	0	972	378
	150	10.21	843	284
215-gr. Lead/ .54-cal. Rifle	0	-	1765	1487
	50	2.44	1207	696
	100	0	951	431
	150	-10.56	820	321

CONICAL BULLETS

Bullet/Rifle Description	Range (Yards)	Impact (Inches)	Velocity (ft./sec.)	Energy (ft./lbs.)
385-gr. Lead/ .50-cal. Rifle	0	-	1360	1582
	50	2.26	1294	1431
	100	0	1179	1187
	150	-8.19	1091	1018
410-gr. Lead/ .50-cal Rifle	0	-	1331	1612
	50	2.34	1263	1452
	100	0	1149	1202
	150	-8.75	1064	1030
425-gr. Lead/ .54-cal. Rifle	0	-	1277	1539
	50	2.58	1208	1376
	100	0	1096	1134
	150	-9.59	1018	977

PERFORMANCE of saboted bullets, conicals and round balls must be considered when developing effective hunting loads. (Many black powder experts feel that about 700 foot-pounds of energy is the minimum for cleanly taking deer and other big game.) The chart above lists bullet impact, velocity and energy for different muzzleloading projectiles when shot from .50- and .54-caliber Knight rifles loaded with 100 grains of FFg black powder.

Note that the only time the .54-caliber rifle shows a real ballistic edge over the .50 is when they are loaded with patched round balls. When the rifles are loaded with conical bullets, the slightly lighter .50-caliber projectile has a bit more velocity and greater energy. And when saboted bullets are fired from either the 50- or .54-caliber muzzleloaders, both produce basically the same velocities and energy levels.

The serious muzzleloading big-game hunter will rely entirely on a much harder-hitting, heavy lead conical or saboted bullet. Loaded with a 100-grain charge of FFg black powder or Pyrodex "RS/Select," a .50-caliber conical bullet of 350 to 400 grains will leave the muzzle (24- to 28-inch barrel) at around 1,400 f.p.s. and generate in the neighborhood of 1,600 foot-pounds of muzzle energy, varying slightly depending on barrel length. At 100 yards, this great hunk of lead will still plow home with nearly 1,200 foot-pounds of energy.

Bullets this heavy do generate a healthy recoil. Another downside to hunting with heavy lead conical bullets is their terrible rainbow trajectory. Out to 100 yards, the bullets shoot relatively flat. Sighted dead-on at 100 yards, most hunting loads with a heavy conical will have a midrange trajectory of about 2½ to 3 inches above point of aim at 50 yards. However, out at 150 yards, some of the heavier bullet designs may drop as much as 9 to 10 inches (p. 52).

More and more, muzzleloading hunters are now turning to the saboted bullets for superior performance on big game. In a sense, these projectiles offer the black powder shooter and hunter the best of both the round ball and the heavy conicals.

The sabot system allows the shooter to load with midweight bullets of 240 to 300 grains. With the same powder charge prescribed for the round ball and conical bullets described above, these bullets deliver muzzle velocities close to those achieved with a patched round ball. On the other hand, being a far superior conical design, the bullets do a much better job of retaining energy downrange. With 100 grains of black powder or Pyrodex, a saboted, 260-grain, .45-caliber jacketed hollow-point bullet will leave the muzzle of a

SIGHT your muzzleloader so you don't have to aim high to compensate for long shots. With a 260-grain, .45-caliber jacketed bullet and 100 grains of black powder or Pyrodex, your bullet impact at 100 yards (●) should be 2 to 3 inches above the aiming point. This will put your shots 3 to 4 inches high at 50 yards (●), and only 2 to 3 inches low at 150 yards ( ).

24-inch barreled in-line percussion rifle at just about 1,600 f.p.s. with close to 1,400 foot-pounds of energy. At 100 yards, the bullet will hit the target with more than 1,000 foot-pounds of energy; at 150 yards, the well-designed, jacketed hollow-point bullet is still good for around 900 foot-pounds of energy.

Sighted to hit dead-on at 100 yards, this load will impact around 1½ inches high at 50 yards. Downrange at 150 yards, the load exhibits right at 6 inches of drop. The shooter who takes the time to sight this load 2 to 3 inches high at 100 yards will find that he or she can pretty well hold dead center of a whitetail buck's chest cavity anywhere from 25 to 150 yards and place a lethal shot into the vitals (above). For bigger game such as elk or bear, saboted bullets of 300 to 325 grains and powder charges of 100 to 110 grains will produce the punch needed for a clean kill.

What kind of accuracy should you expect from your muzzleloader? Truth is, most of today's quality muzzleloading rifles can produce better accuracy than most of us are capable of shooting. A few of today's rifle manufacturers claim that their guns are able to produce 1½-inch groups at 100 yards when loaded and fired with their prescribed loads. If you have aspirations of competing in target matches on a national level, start honing your shooting skills. At the National Muzzle Loading Rifle Association matches held

TAP the side of the powder measure to ensure that it is completely empty.

AVOID pounding and deforming a projectile with a hammer or ramrod.

WIPE the bore clean of black powder fouling between each shot.

at Friendship, Indiana, several times each year, national champions of the different matches are sometimes determined by actual measurement of holes in the targets. It's not uncommon for some bench-rest matches to end with three, four or five shooters achieving perfect scores. The shooter with shots closest to dead center is the winner.

While winning one of these prestigious matches requires the shooter to be as exact as humanly possible, hunting accuracy is a little more forgiving. If you can keep your hits inside of 3 or 4 inches at whatever distance you feel is your maximum effective range with the rifle you're shooting, and you are shooting a load that develops adequate energy levels, you should be able to cleanly harvest whatever big game you are hunting.

Loading Practices

Good loading practices at the bench and in the field are extremely important to developing an accurate load. Always treat every load as if it is a custom handload, because it really is! Every time you measure a powder charge, pour it down the barrel, start a projectile and seat it over the powder charge, you are building a load that's been tailored to your muzzleloader. Do it the same each and every time – right down to the amount of pressure you place on the ramrod when seating the projectile – and your reward will be better accuracy.

There are no shortcuts to better performance with a muzzleloading rifle. Before loading any rifle, always make sure that it isn't already loaded (see Loading Tip, p. 72). Then, before pouring a powder charge down the barrel, take time to wipe the bore clean of any oil left from a previous cleaning. Next, make sure that the ignition system is clear and that fire from the priming pan of a flintlock or from the percussion cap of a caplock gun will reach the powder charge. When measuring the powder charge, tap the side of the measure as it fills to ensure that you have the same amount of powder in each charge (above). Take your time pouring it into the bore and try to avoid spilling even a few granules. The same care should be taken when starting the projectile. Remember that a ball or bullet that's damaged during loading will hamper accuracy. Last, but not least, seat your chosen projectile over the powder charge with the same amount of pressure for each shot.

For best accuracy with any rifle or projectile, wipe the bore free of fouling between each shot. Black powder fouling builds more quickly than the fouling left behind from Pyrodex, but the fouling from either propellant can and will affect accuracy. Competition shooters meticulously wipe the bore between each shot. On the other hand, hunters may take the time when working up loads at the shooting bench, but don't want to be bothered with wiping the bore when trying to quickly reload a follow-up shot in the field. When it comes to maintaining hunting accuracy with a fouled bore, loads developed with Pyrodex are much more forgiving than those with black powder.

Cleaning Muzzleloaders

No matter what style of frontloading gun you own, when you shoot it, you've just committed yourself to cleaning it. It's that simple. That charming, billowing white cloud that hangs at the muzzle also leaves behind a dirty, smelly mess in the bore. The prospect of having to clean that out has typically caused apprehension among first-time black powder shooters – it need not.

Once you understand what that dirty, smelly residue can do to damage your muzzleloader, compared to how cheaply and thoroughly you can clean all the parts in less than a half hour, you'll get rid of any apprehension you may have had. Cleaning and care will become as natural and important to you as your loading and shooting skills.

Both black powder and Pyrodex are very corrosive. It doesn't matter if you've fired your frontloader once during the course of a day's hunt, or a dozen or more times sighting in at the range; if the gun has been fired it MUST be cleaned thoroughly before the day is over. Fouling left in a barrel overnight can be enough to totally ruin the bore forever. This is especially true during really damp weather, or if you happen to live in a very humid climate.

The fouling left behind by burning charges of either black powder or Pyrodex is extremely hygroscopic; it will literally pull moisture out of the air. During shooting, the heat from burning powder removes all traces of any protective lubricant from the surface of the bore. The corrosive fouling begins to work immediately on the unprotected metal surface and,

on a damp day, can cause rust in the bore over the span of a single afternoon. Left uncleaned overnight, the highest-quality and most accurate muzzleloading barrel can be reduced to little more than scrap metal.

Don't be fooled by guns that feature stainless steel barrels and other major metal parts. Stainless steel buys you time when shooting and hunting in wet weather, but once it has been coated with black powder or Pyrodex fouling, it has to be cleaned just as meticulously as a blued-steel muzzleloader.

What to do? It's easy. Both black powder and Pyrodex fouling can be cleaned out of a muzzleloaders's bore with nothing more than good ol' hot, soapy water. In fact, residue left behind by either powder can be scrubbed away using just water, hot or cold. Soap will speed up the cleaning process, especially if your loads were round balls with lubed patches or heavy lead conical bullets liberally lubricated. Using hot water during the cleaning process heats the metal of the barrel and speeds up drying when it's time to wipe internal and external metal surfaces.

Any good liquid dishwashing detergent with hot water makes an excellent solution for cleaning your favorite muzzleloader. Use about the same amount you would when washing the dishes from an evening meal. One word of caution: wet black powder or Pyrodex fouling emits an odor that's similar to the smell of rotten eggs. You may want to remain in good standing with the family by cleaning your muzzleloader outside.

A number of the traditionally styled side-hammer rifle and shotgun models feature a barrel with a hooked breech system. As the name implies, these barrels have a hook-shaped extension at the rear of the breech plug that fits into a recessed metal piece attached to the stock. To remove a hooked breech barrel from the stock assembly, tap out a wedge or pin running through the forestock and the tenon loop attached to the bottom of the barrel. A special tool called a *wedge puller* (below) is designed specifically for removing these tight-fitting wedges. The barrel can then be lifted from the stock.

The easiest way to clean a hooked breech barrel is to submerge the breech end of the barrel into a container of hot, soapy water. Next, thread a cleaning jag into one end of a ramrod. Then, dampen a cleaning patch, place it over the bore and push it on into the barrel with the ramrod and cleaning jag. Push the patch to the bottom of the bore, then pull it back toward the muzzle. This creates a suction through the vent hole of a flintlock barrel or through the flash channel of a percussion gun's nipple. The hot, soapy water is sucked into the barrel as the patch is pulled toward the muzzle, then forced out again as the patch is shoved back toward the breech end. Several

dozen strokes of the ramrod free the bore of black powder fouling.

Wipe the outside of the barrel dry immediately with paper towels or a dry towel. Four or five dry patches up and down the bore usually wipe away any moisture. If the water was relatively hot, the metal should be very warm to the touch. Let the barrel air dry further while you wipe away fouling from other parts of the gun, such as the hammer and lock plate, or the hooked breech recess at the rear of the barrel channel. The heated metal rapidly dries moisture left in the bore.

Once you're sure the bore and the outside of the barrel are dry, spray a cleaning patch liberally with a good moisture displacing oil and run it down the bore. Oil the outside of the barrel as well. Wipe excess oil from the bore by running a couple of dry patches down the barrel; then wipe the outside of the barrel with a dry cloth. The rifle is ready to be reassembled.

To oil or not to oil – this is a question that has caused debate among hunters for decades. A large number of black powder shooters shun the practice of putting oil in the bore. Many feel that it is flirting with disaster the next time the muzzleloader is

How to Clean Removable Barrels

REMOVE the wedge in the forestock with a wedge puller.

LIFT the barrel off the stock and prepare a bucket of hot, soapy water.

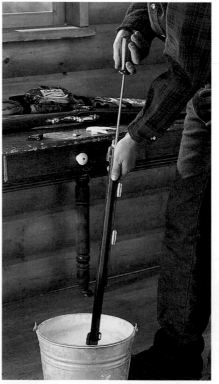

FORCE the soapy water in and out of the barrel by working a cleaning patch back and forth. After the fouling has been removed, wipe the outside of the barrel with paper towels.

SPRAY a cleaning patch with moisture displacing oil. After the bore has dried, run the oiled patch down the bore. Finish by using a few dry patches in the bore to remove excess oil.

loaded. It's true that oil in the ignition system has probably caused more misfires than anything else. But excess oil in the bore can be wiped free with a few dry patches, and the ignition system can be easily cleared before the rifle is loaded again.

Remember, the fouling left behind from burning loads of both black powder and Pyrodex will draw moisture right out of the air. Even a muzzleloader bore that seems perfectly clean can still leave a few specks of burnt fouling carbon in some of the pores of the metal. A good coat of oil in the bore seals these minute deposits off from the air and prevents the tiny bit of fouling left behind from pulling moisture from the air and causing light rust in the barrel. Many veteran black powder shooters use cleaning patches seasoned with a natural lube (right) to protect the bore.

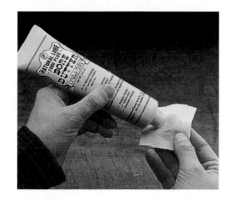

There are a number of muzzleloader barrels that do not feature a hooked breech system and are not designed to be removed. The easiest method for cleaning these is to use a flush tube – a flexible piece of small-diameter rubber tubing through which the soapy water cleaning solution can be pulled by the suction of the tight-fitting patch and cleaning jag. Flush tubes are also an easy option for hunters who prefer not to remove the barrel of their favorite muzzleloader for cleaning (below).

Several suppliers sell flush tubes for percussion guns. These are attached easily by removing the nipple from the gun and threading in a brass adapter to which the rubber tubing is affixed. For flintlock guns, there is a similar arrangement that clamps onto the barrel and aligns the end of the tube with the vent hole.

With a flush tube attached to the muzzleloader, drop the loose end of the tubing (about 14 or 15 inches in length) into a container of hot, soapy water. Next, place a damp cleaning patch over the muzzle of the gun and push into the bore with the cleaning jag of your ramrod. The bore is then cleaned in the same manner as the hooked breech barrel, except that the barrel stays connected to the stock assembly.

How to Use a Flush Tube

REMOVE the nipple of a percussion caplock muzzleloader.

THREAD the brass adapter of the flush tube onto the muzzleloader.

PLACE the other end of the flush tube in a bucket of hot, soapy water. A hole cut in the plastic cover of the bucket aids in holding the tube in place.

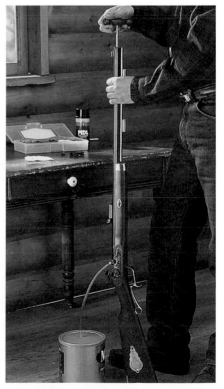

DRAW the water from the bucket and into the barrel by creating suction with a cleaning patch attached to a ramrod. Finish by drying and oiling the barrel.

97

REMOVE the hammer assembly from the back of the receiver.

UNSCREW and remove the nipple and breech plug from the barrel.

WORK cleaning patches that have been dampened with black powder solvent through the barrel and receiver.

Modern in-line percussion rifles featuring a removable breech plug are without a doubt the most user-friendly muzzleloaders available. Those makes and models designed for complete teardown are supplied with a special tool that removes the nipple and breech plug from the rear of the barrel. The barrel is then open on each end, allowing the shooter to clean the frontloader straight through, in the same manner as cleaning a modern centerfire (above).

Not only does the removable breech plug of most in-line rifles make cleaning a much simpler task, it provides easy access to the barrel and ignition system. This is convenient if you forget to load powder before seating the projectile or experience a misfire due to damp or contaminated powder. After a day of hunting, one of these rifles can be easily unloaded by removing the breech plug and pushing the powder and bullet out the back with the ramrod (right). It beats shooting out the load and having to give the muzzleloader a thorough cleaning to scrub out residue left from a burnt powder charge.

An alternative to cleaning with hot, soapy water is to rely on any number of top-quality black powder cleaning solvents. These have been formulated to efficiently break down black powder or Pyrodex fouling. Although most do an excellent job, the task

of cleaning the fouling from the bore can require ramrodding quite a few solvent-saturated patches before one finally comes out clean. Once the bore is clean, several dry patches are run down the bore, followed by a liberal coat of oil.

The corrosive effect of black powder or Pyrodex fouling is obviously not confined to the barrel alone. Now let's turn our attention to the equally important cleaning and care of the "other" surfaces of your muzzleloader that are susceptible to fouling degradation. The nose of a percussion hammer nearly always features a recess to prevent cap particles from flying back and hitting the shooter or bystanders. It's an ideal place for fouling to accumulate. The lock plate just below the nipple of a percussion gun or around the pan of a flintlock can't help but be dusted with fouling. You will also find a significant amount of powder fouling inside the receiver of an in-line percussion muzzleloader. These are the main areas needing inspection and cleaning but you will want to make sure all fouling is removed wherever it is discovered.

A toothbrush makes an excellent cleaning tool for carefully scrubbing residue from the nose of a percussion hammer and lock plates (opposite page). A bore brush is well suited for rapidly removing fouling from the inside of an in-line rifle receiver. Besides being simple and effective, a toothbrush and bore brush allow you to control the amount of hot, soapy water solution or black powder solvent you are applying. It is essential that you be careful not to get your cleaning solution down inside components such as the lock mechanism of a traditional side-hammer or the trigger assemblies of traditional

How to Clean Other Surfaces

BRUSH the nose of a percussion gun's hammer to remove fouling caused by fired percussion caps.

SCRUB a flintlock's flash pan to get rid of the residue left from burnt priming powder.

LOOSEN black powder fouling from an in-line muzzleloader's receiver with a bore brush.

or modern in-line percussion frontloaders. These components and assemblies were not intended to come apart and only require a little wiping and oiling from time to time.

Most muzzleloading long guns can be cleaned using one of these methods. Manuals and instructions included with new muzzleloaders also detail features or steps to aid in cleaning a particular model.

Modern-day copies of the famed Colt cap and ball revolvers must be completely disassembled for cleaning (below). They are designed with removable barrel assemblies and cylinders that slip from a pin. In a matter of a minute or two, one of these hand-guns can be broken down into three major parts groups – the frame, the barrel and the cylinder.

The design of Remington-style percussion revolvers allows the cylinder to be removed for cleaning, but the barrel stays solidly attached to the frame. To clean the barrel, simply hold the revolver with the muzzle pointing downward. This will keep any of the cleaning solution from getting into the internal mechanism.

The shooting of any muzzleloading gun is a binding commitment that you'll properly clean that muzzleloader. One thing is for certain, a muzzleloader that is properly cleaned and cared for will function and perform properly the next time you are ready to use it. Wouldn't it be nice to leave your children something other than a rusted, nonfunctioning wall hanger?

How to Clean Revolvers

COLT-STYLE REVOLVERS are designed so both the barrel and cylinder detach from the frame.

REMINGTON-STYLE REVOLVERS are built so the cylinder detaches from the frame but the barrel does not.

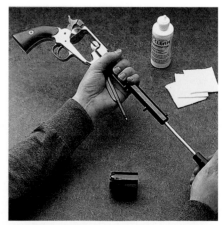

SOLVENTS should be kept from running into the internal parts by cleaning with the muzzle pointing downward.

Hunting with Muzzleloaders

Whitetail Deer

If you're just now getting into muzzleloading to take advantage of bonus hunting opportunities offered by the special muzzleloading whitetail deer season or seasons held in many states, you're not alone. The lure of these so-called primitive seasons has brought more new participants into muzzleloading than any other reason, creating one of the fastest-growing segments of shooting and hunting sports.

A survey of all new deer hunting opportunities in the U.S. over the past 20 years reveals that most have been either the establishment or expansion of muzzleloading seasons. There is a terrific win-win reason for this. Whitetail populations have exploded everywhere. A growing number of state game departments have responded by relying on muzzleloading hunts and seasons to increase the harvest. As a result, muzzleloading hunters are now playing an important role in the management of our burgeoning whitetail herd.

The dedicated whitetail hunter couldn't be happier with these circumstances. If you're like most deer hunters, you simply can't seem to get in enough hunting during the archery and general firearms seasons. Today, muzzleloading offers an honest "third season" opportunity, causing hunters everywhere to turn to frontloading guns in record numbers.

In most states, general firearms seasons give a trophy hunter a great chance to put his tag on a wall hanger. These seasons usually take place during the rut, or mating season, when bucks tend to be the most active.

There is some variation in the timing of the rut from north to south, but not a great deal. For instance, the peak of the rut in Saskatchewan, Canada, falls about the same time as the peak of the rut in Iowa, Missouri, Illinois and a number of other states. Whitetail hunting seasons coincide with these time periods. This can create a problem for hunters planning to hunt in three or four different states. Thanks to muzzleload-

ing seasons, hunters have discovered that they can more than double the amount of time spent afield pursuing whitetails.

Only a handful of muzzleloader seasons actually take place during the peak of the rut. More states schedule their muzzleloader deer hunts after the general firearms season instead of before. However, a growing number of states now conduct two separate (before and after) muzzleloading deer seasons (right). Each of these represent advantages and disadvantages in relationship to the general firearms season in between and the use of a muzzleloader.

Some states offer both early and late muzzleloader deer seasons

Early season whitetail hunters are faced with thick foliage

Late season hunters often battle deep snow and bitter cold

Hunting during the early muzzleloader seasons can be rewarding, but these hunts can also be extremely tough. One advantage of an early season is that most take place during the month of October, well before the really cold weather sets in and before the army of modern gun hunters hits the deer woods, spooking the naturally nervous whitetails to the point of being afraid of their own shadow. Except for a few encounters with bowhunters, early muzzleloader season whitetails have seen very little hunting pressure. At this time of the year, if you can get onto a good buck, establish some definite travel patterns and have the patience to wait the deer out, there is a very good chance that sooner or later that buck will waltz right in front of your sights.

A disadvantage of many early muzzleloading seasons is that food is abundant everywhere. An ol' buck just doesn't have to travel very far at all to fill his stomach, especially if the ground is covered with white oak acorns. In mid- to late October, the foliage is usually still pretty heavy (left). Shots at whitetails in the timber are often restricted to less than 50 yards due to the fact that you just can't see any farther. On the other hand, deer are more plentiful before the harvest of the general firearms season, and if you're satisfied to harvest a lesser buck or doe, the early muzzleloading seasons are a great time to be in the deer woods.

If you're looking to tag a big buck with your muzzleloader, you may want to know that most expert muzzleloading whitetail hunters tend to favor the late muzzleloading seasons. For one thing, these seasons are usually the most underhunted of the year. The hordes of fluorescent-orange-coated centerfire-toting whitetail hunters who filled the deer woods during the regular gun season are by then spending all of their free time living up to holiday commitments or watching football on television. For the knowledgeable whitetail hunter who simply isn't ready to hang it up for the year, the late frontloader whitetail seasons in many states can be extremely productive. Two obvious keys to being successful at this time of the year are to be able to spend enough time in the woods to learn where to find whitetails and to rely on a rifle that will effectively reach out when you need it to perform.

December and early January can produce some very unpredictable weather – a major factor in why late seasons don't have a great deal of hunting pressure. In the South, this can be a very rainy period, as warmer Gulf air pushes northward. Throughout the North, Midwest and New England states, winter has set in (left). When plummeting temperatures produce bitter cold and snow blankets the ground, a whitetail's instincts turn from breeding (as the rut winds down) to sheer survival.

Whitetail buck feeding in a standing cornfield

Adverse weather conditions dictate where the muzzle-loading hunter concentrates his search for whitetails. Does normally come through the rut in pretty good condition, but active bucks may have lost much needed body weight. Food becomes their number one priority (above).

This isn't to say that all rutting activity is over by early December. Not all does enter the first estrus period at the same time. A time span of a couple of weeks between the earliest to the latest doe to come into heat will keep an old buck running from wood-lot to woodlot.

The buck-to-doe ratio is lopsided in most whitetail country: there may be only one mature buck for every 10 to 15 does. Consequently, quite a few does come out of the primary rut without ever having been bred. Many late muzzleloader seasons allow the hunter to harvest a buck or doe, making these seasons a great time to put some venison in the freezer.

These same does will once again enter estrus about 30 days later. This period is commonly referred to as the *secondary rut*. Not surprisingly, in the North, upper Midwest and along the upper East Coast, this secondary rut usually takes place at about the same time as many late muzzleloader seasons.

Even though the second rut period can provide some great whitetail action, especially where hunting pressure is practically nonexistent during a late muzzleloader season, rut patterns definitely begin to taper off quickly as the year reaches its end. By mid-December, deer in northern zones begin to bunch together as survival becomes the major concern. At this time of year, most whitetail movement is directed toward strategic food sources. Where temperatures can plummet to -20° or -30°F, with windchill factors pushing -60°F, whitetails have to feed in order to generate body heat. While you're not likely to see a big buck throw all caution to the wind by gluttonously filling his stomach with cornfield remnants right out in broad daylight, you can narrow your search for whitetails by concentrating on known feed areas. Where grain crops are common, whitetails are generally close at hand; in heavily timbered regions, concentrate where the mast crop was the heaviest. In the west, bottomland hay fields can be a big draw.

The colder the weather, the more difficult it is for equipment to function – muzzleloading rifles are certainly no exception. Be aware that when temperatures drop way below freezing, the otherwise smooth-working mechanics of your muzzleloader may suddenly freeze up. There are do's and don'ts to circumvent this occurrence in advance.

Many black powder hunters try to cold-weatherize the lock, trigger and other moving parts of their muzzleloader by liberally applying oil or high-tech gun greases. More often than not, this only creates greater problems. Any time oil or grease is applied to moving parts, cold weather can make metal surfaces sticky. Moving parts that are sluggish result in a malfunctioning trigger or a lock mechanism that drops the hammer too slowly and lightly to snap a percussion cap. Naturally, traditional side-hammer muzzleloaders are more susceptible to the ill effects of cold weather than the newer in-line percussion rifles.

Whenever you hunt in sub-zero temperatures, you should prepare your muzzleloader by using a good cleaning solvent or alcohol to totally degrease the surfaces of moving parts (below). Then spray a cloth sparingly with a light machine oil or one of the newer Teflon®-based gun oils, and lightly wipe the metal surfaces with it. Lastly, wipe these surfaces with a dry cloth. The idea is to leave just enough lubricant on the metal to prevent corrosion, but not enough to hamper the function of the mechanism during cold-weather use.

The serious whitetail hunter who braves extremely cold weather for one last crack at a good buck won't entrust the success of the hunt to just any muzzleloader. It's a good bet he or she will be packing one of the deadly accurate in-line percussion rifles, and where legal, that rifle will be fitted with a good scope. Where a late season hunt regularly coincides with rainy or snowy weather, bolt-action rifles like the Remington Model 700ML or the Austin & Halleck with a weather shroud installed at the face of the bolt will keep the percussion cap protected from the moisture, insuring good ignition when a heavy horned buck suddenly appears.

Late-season whitetail hunting can also mean shots that can be on the long side, and for optimum performance most modern, scoped in-line rifles will be loaded with an equally modern saboted bullet.

How to Cold-weatherize Muzzleloaders

DEGREASE the surfaces of the gun's moving parts with solvent or alcohol.

SPRAY a patch with a Teflon-based oil and lightly wipe the moving parts.

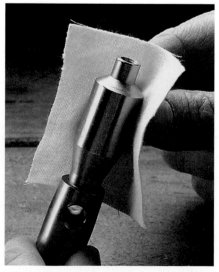

WIPE these same surfaces with a dry patch to remove any excess oil.

Jacketed pistol bullets or one of the newer all copper muzzleloading bullets like the Barnes Expander-MZ of 250 to 300 grains are ideal choices. When loaded ahead of 90 to 110 grains of FFg black powder or Pyrodex "RS/Select" (or two 50-grain Pyrodex pellets), such a load develops tremendous energy levels and, for a muzzleloader, shoots extremely flat.

The hefty three 50-grain Pyrodex pellet loads (150-grain charge) now being promoted by Knight, Thompson/Center, and a few other manufacturers, flatten out muzzleloader trajectory even more, and deliver a well-designed modern saboted bullet with quite a wallop all the way out to 200 yards. Saboted .44- and .45-caliber bullets of 240 to 250 grains are pushed from the muzzle at more than 2,000 f.p.s., with energy levels surpassing those of some centerfire rifles. And the new Savage Model 10ML, which has been designed to shoot smokeless powder loads, ups muzzle velocity of a saboted 250-grain bullet to nearly 2,300 f.p.s. Sighted dead-on at 100 yards, the load prints just 2 inches low at 150, and less than 5 inches low at 200 yards. To better contain the higher pressures of such hotter loads, the Savage rifle is built with a fully enclosed ignition system, which also keeps out all moisture.

The effectiveness of the modern in-line rifles and saboted bullet loads is now making them more popular during the general firearms seasons, as well. This is especially true in more than 20 states where regulations require the use of modern shotguns and slugs during the regular firearms seasons. The outstanding accuracy of a scoped, in-line rifle at 100 to 150 yards actually makes the muzzleloader a better choice than most modern shotguns. You may have only one shot, but with one of these muzzleloading rifles, you can put it exactly where you want it to go.

Other Big Game

North American big-game animals basically fall into one of two categories – (1) those the same size as or slightly smaller than whitetails, and (2) those larger than whitetails. This is an appropriate way for muzzleloading hunters to classify big game in order to develop loads that will cleanly take whatever they are hunting.

Not all big-game animals are necessarily big. For example, javelinas (often called *collared peccary*) of the Southwest rarely weigh more than 60 pounds. In fact, in much of their range, a 50-pounder is considered a large trophy. Then we have the petite Coues' whitetails of the desert regions of Arizona, New Mexico and old Mexico, whose really big bucks might push 100 pounds. And then, there's the pronghorn of the American West with exceptionally large bucks still weighing no more than 125 pounds live weight. Any muzzleloading rifle load that will cleanly take a big northern whitetail or good, average-sized mule deer is actually overkill on big game this size.

Muzzleloading hunters going after really big game, such as elk, moose, caribou and larger bears, should rely on a rifle of large-enough caliber and a load healthy enough to ensure that it will do the job. Some of the states offering participation in a separate muzzleloader hunt for elk have already eliminated the option of going after this big deer with anything less than a .50-caliber frontloader. There is also now a move toward establishing minimum projectile weights in some areas, making it illegal to hunt elk with a .50-caliber loaded with a patched round ball.

The concern is that even rifles of .50-caliber loaded with a soft lead ball of 175 to 180 grains will not develop enough energy to guarantee a clean, humane kill on an animal topping a half ton in weight. Saboted bullets of 300 to 400 grains and heavy lead conical bullets of near 400 to around 500 grains will smack an elk at 100 yards with two to three times more energy than a round ball fired from the same-caliber rifle (p. 91).

One of the first things the eastern hunter headed west will have to learn to cope with is the openness

Rocky Mountain bighorn ram

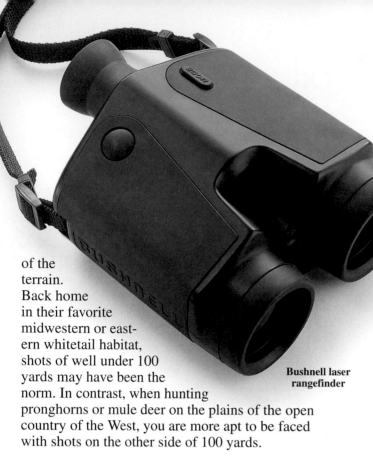

Bushnell laser rangefinder

of the terrain. Back home in their favorite midwestern or eastern whitetail habitat, shots of well under 100 yards may have been the norm. In contrast, when hunting pronghorns or mule deer on the plains of the open country of the West, you are more apt to be faced with shots on the other side of 100 yards.

So, what is the maximum effective range of a muzzle-loading hunting rifle? Actually, most .50- and .54-caliber rifles loaded with a hefty powder charge and an aerodynamically superior conical bullet (either saboted handgun bullets or heavy lead bore-sized conical projectiles) will maintain plenty of knock-down energy out to, and slightly past, 200 yards. However, unless you are an experienced shooter at those distances, limiting shots to a maximum of 150 yards is a more effective practice.

A 50-caliber rifle loaded with a 385-grain Hornady Great Plains bullet or Buffalo Bullet Company hollow-pointed "Maxi Bullet" that has been sighted in with 100 grains of FFg black powder or Pyrodex "RS/Select" to print on at 100 yards will drop to about 8 inches below point of aim at 150 yards (p. 52). Most hunters learn to allow for that much drop, and do a fair job of estimating range out to 150 yards.

From 150 to 200 yards, this same load will drop an additional 18 or so inches. That's right, from 100 to 200 yards, the heavy lead conical bullet will drop a full 26 inches, with more than two-thirds of that drop in trajectory occurring in the last 50 yards. The hunter who misjudges by 20 yards the distance of a big-game animal at 200 yards will end up with a bad hit that could be as much as 6 to 8 inches high or low. Saboted bullets of 300 to 325 grains are still plenty big for taking out even the largest North American game and will flatten trajectory by as much as 6 inches out at 200 yards. Still, it takes an experienced hunter who is a great judge of distance

to ethically attempt such long-range shots at game with a muzzleloader.

One of the handiest devices the muzzleloading hunter can own is one of the modern laser rangefinders (left). Some of today's models are far lighter than a pair of binoculars and are precise to within a yard or two. To use, a hunter simply sights in on a distant target, pushes a button and, before he can release the button, the rangefinder will tell him the exact distance to the target. Knowing the exact range is critical when shooting muzzle-loaders at distances past 150 yards.

Remember, the bigger the animal, the more energy required to do the job well. The bullet used to down a frail pronghorn cannot cleanly down a huge, 2,000-pound bull moose, for example. If you are bound and determined to take really big game with a tradition-ally styled muzzleloader and a patched round ball, use something big. When hunting game as large as elk with the patched round ball, consider a .54-caliber bore size as your absolute minimum. With 100 to 110 grains of FFg black powder or Pyrodex "RS/Select" behind a 230-grain, .530-inch round ball, a 26- to 28-inch barreled Hawken-style rifle will develop around 1,700 foot-pounds of energy at the muzzle. However, by the time that ball gets to 100 yards, it's only good for around 650 foot-pounds of energy. Keeping shots well within 100 yards is crucial to ensuring that there will be adequate energy remain-ing to take an animal this big.

Today you'll find muzzleloading hunters heading in all directions of North America in pursuit of every big-game hunting opportunity (right). Trophies, once thought to be exclusively for the centerfire hunter who could afford the costly price tag of such a hunt, are now being harvested with a muzzleloader by hunters who wouldn't even have considered picking up a frontloading rifle just 10 or 20 years ago.

The confidence today's hunter has in the newer in-line percussion rifles and saboted bullets is a major factor in why many of these hunters have turned to muzzle-loading. So is the challenge of the "one-shot" hunt. Another influence is the establishment of a separate record book for muzzleloader-harvested big-game trophies (see The Longhunter, p. 123). Administered by the National Muzzle Loading Rifle Association, the record book offers serious trophy-minded hunters an excellent opportunity "to get into the book." The minimum qualifying scores for all North American big-game species fall somewhere between those established for the Pope and Young Club archery record book and the Boone and Crockett Club record book.

Wild Turkey

More than a dozen muzzleloading shotguns on the market are well suited to hunting America's big game bird – the wild turkey. A number of recent introductions are designed with the serious turkey hunter in mind, featuring a tight choke at the muzzle to create turkey-taking patterns out to about 35 yards.

At the same time, there are still a few faithful reproductions of original muzzleloading shotgun designs built without chokes of any sort. These cylinder-bored smoothbores are capable of throwing nice, even patterns if you are willing to take a little extra time with your loading procedures.

The first step to obtaining the best patterns from any muzzleloading shotgun begins with loading as nearly equal volumes of powder and shot as possible. (In some shotgun bores, the ratio of one to the other may vary slightly for best performance.) This is because a heavy powder charge and light shot charge, or vice versa, seldom produces the game-getting pattern densities needed to make sure that an old gobbler will be on the ground when the smoke clears.

It's a fact that open-choked muzzleloading shotguns simply can't match a choked smoothbore for reaching out farther to dump a big 20-pound-plus gobbler. But don't let that deter you. By taking the time to use the proper sequence of wads during loading (p. 74), along with enough powder and shot to do the job, you can produce patterns that will easily take a gobbler that gets within range of the business end of your muzzleloading scattergun (below).

Even a skillfully crafted load won't tighten the pattern of a cylinder-bored shotgun. However, by taking the time to load with nearly equal volumes of powder and shot, along with the correct sequence of wads, you'll find that you can improve the evenness of your patterns with more pellets toward the center.

Tight choke constriction at the muzzle makes it nearly impossible to stuff properly fitted wads through it so that the wads will also fit the bore correctly after stuffing. The newer smoothbores, built with removable screw-in chokes, eliminate this problem. The choke is simply removed before loading and replaced after all of the ingredients have been stuffed in.

Taking it one step further, the real advantage of removable chokes on most modern muzzleloading shotguns means that these guns can be loaded with a one-piece plastic wad (such as those used in loading shotshells for breechloading shotguns). The reduction in loading time is significant, maximizing second shot possibilities.

Comparing Shot Load Patterns at Different Distances

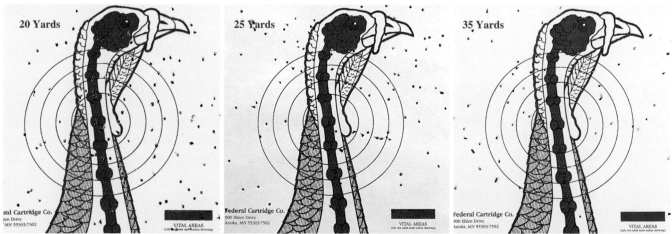

KILLING shots at a turkey require at least three pellets in the vital (red) zone of the head and neck. At 20 yards, the pattern above puts over a dozen pellets in the vitals. At 25 and 35 yards, the pattern widens and fewer pellets strike the vitals. Your maximum shooting range, usually 35 to 40 yards, is the distance when fewer than three pellets consistently hit the vital zone.

Equipped with a full or extra-full choke threaded back into the muzzle of the shotgun, one of these smoothbores will pattern as well as any 3-inch, magnum, 12-gauge, breechloading turkey shotgun. The softer push of the black powder or Pyrodex can actually result in patterns that display better center density than is possible with the smokeless turkey loads in a modern shotgun.

Several in-line percussion caplocks and a couple of the more traditionally styled side-by-side muzzle-loading shotguns on the market feature removable screw-in chokes. These are ideal choices for hunting wild turkey.

A large number of states have wild turkey hunts during the fall months, but for dedicated turkey hunters there is only one real season: spring. At this time of the year, thunderous gobbles of mature toms trying to attract a receptive hen fill the spring hardwoods. Woods-wise muzzleloading hunters learn to master the subtle calls of the wild turkey hen to lure even the craftiest old gobbler to within range of their muzzleloading shotguns.

April showers bring May flowers, but the wet weather too often accompanying spring turkey seasons can also make a muzzleloading hunt a more challenging time afield. Without a doubt, wet and rainy weather is the muzzleloading turkey hunter's number one nemesis – and that's why it is important to know how to beat it.

You can't hunt confidently if your mind is filled with doubts about whether or not your shotgun will fire once you have coaxed a gobbler within range. Muzzle-loading guns are definitely affected by damp weather. That's why serious black powder hunters take several precautions to greatly reduce the possibilities of a misfire long before they go afield. You can, too.

Dealing with Rainy Weather

Before loading your shotgun, run several dry patches down the bore to remove oil from the last cleaning. Also, under extremely damp conditions, high humidity levels can actually result in a minute amount of moisture in the barrel itself. This is especially true if the gun is left stored in the trunk of a car or in any unheated area. A couple of passes with dry, soft cotton patches will wipe the bore bone-dry.

Now, go through the normal routine of snapping two or three caps to clear the nipple (or nipples, if the gun happens to be a double). This will also ensure that the flash channel leading from the nipple to the barrel is clear and dry, as well. When snapping a cap on the nipple, it is a good idea to use the ramrod and cleaning jag to push a dry patch down the barrel and leave it sitting at the face of the breech plug. Oil that may be in the flash channel is then thrown onto the patch instead of into the barrel. Also, if your ignition system is putting adequate fire into the barrel, you'll find a burnt spot on the patch.

Tips for Hunting in Rainy Weather

PLACE your capper in an airtight Ziplock® bag to protect the percussion caps from moisture.

DAB lube on the bottom of a cushion wad (left), or into the base of a plastic wad (right). The lube spreads to form a waterproof barrier after the wad is seated against an over-powder card in the barrel.

114

Black powder and Pyrodex will absorb moisture from the air, so always keep your powder stored in an airtight container. Most flasks are far from being airtight. If you know that you'll be hunting in damp weather, leave your flask at home and carry your powder charges in speed load tubes with weathertight, snap-on plastic caps (p. 65). Speed loaders that feature two separate compartments are perfect for carrying loads for the muzzleloading shotgun. Most have compartments of identical size, allowing plenty of room for 90 to 110 grains of FFg or Pyrodex "RS/Select" powder and 2 ounces of No. 4, 5 or 6 shot. Three or four of these in a jacket pocket, and you're ready for a morning hunt.

When loading with traditional card and fiber cushion wads, you can easily seal the main powder charge from wet weather by squirting a dab of black powder lube on the bottom of the cushion wad. When this is seated over the over-powder card, the lube will spread evenly to form a waterproof barrier.

If you happen to be hunting with a modern muzzleloading shotgun with a choke system and loading with the one-piece plastic wads, you may want to load a heavy over-powder card directly over the powder charge and then squirt a little black powder lube into the cupped base of the plastic wad. This will keep moisture from seeping into the powder charge from the muzzle end of the shotgun. Muzzle covers also help keep moisture from reaching the powder.

Misfires with percussion muzzleloaders are more often due to the percussion cap, rather than the powder charge, getting wet. In really damp weather you should keep your capper in a Ziplock® bag and replace the cap on the gun with a fresh, dry one whenever you suspect that moisture has reached the cap. However, if you know you're faced with a real "toad strangler," waterproofing the ignition system is a must.

Several companies now offer nipple and cap protectors that work fairly well to protect the ignition system in a downpour, but dampness may still seep in. A simple remedy is to rely on a light coat of beeswax or bowstring wax to waterproof the cap and nipple. Lightly coat the outside cone of the nipple, taking precautions not to get any of the wax down inside the nipple. Then press the cap tightly into place on the nipple, and follow up by rubbing a little more wax around the bottom edge of the cap. This will keep the cap and nipple dry all day, no matter how soaked you may get.

The challenge of hunting the wild turkey with a muzzleloading shotgun is to lure a wary ol' gobbler to within the effective range of the smoothbore you're carrying. If it's one of the open-choked reproductions of the scatterguns from the mid-1800s, that means getting the big bird to within 15 or 20 yards. Hunting the wild turkey with a muzzleloading shotgun can get "up close and personal."

STRETCH a muzzle cover over the end of the barrel to keep rain out. You can shoot right through the cover.

Cap guard

SEAT a cap guard over the base of the percussion cap to prevent moisture from entering from below.

COAT the edges of the percussion cap with bowstring wax (above) or beeswax to keep the cap dry.

Small Game

To be considered a true small-game muzzleloading rifle, a frontloader has to have a small bore. Even though the selection of .32- and .36-caliber squirrel rifles isn't nearly as great as the variety of larger-bore muzzleloaders for bigger game, there are a number of well-made small-caliber guns for the hunter looking to try his hand at potting a few bushytails or sniping at cottontails.

There never has been a bore size that could be considered the all-purpose caliber; one that's ideal for taking both small and deer-sized game. Even the .45-caliber rifles, which are considered borderline effective on whitetails and similarly sized game, are way too large for something as small as a squirrel. Even with light 20- to 30-grain powder charges behind a .440- or .445-inch patched round ball, rifles this size are still way too destructive for use on small game. After all, the idea is to take home meat for the table.

Smallbore muzzleloaders of .32- or .36-caliber can still be a little destructive when stoked up with hefty powder charges. When loading one of these pipsqueak bored muzzleloaders, remember that you're not out to develop as much energy as possible. It doesn't take a lot of punch to tumble a squirrel out of the branches overhead, or to drop a rabbit that's sunning itself on a winter's day. But, it does take a very accurately placed shot to prevent ruining a lot of edible meat.

Powder charges of 30 to 40 grains are a waste in a rifle that's being loaded for small-game hunting. Many experienced muzzleloading squirrel hunters rely on just 15 to 20 grains of FFFg black powder or Pyrodex "P" grade behind a .310- to .315-inch patched round ball. This will push one of the 44- to 47-grain soft lead spheres out of the muzzle at about 1,300 f.p.s. and develop more energy than a .22 centerfire rifle. The .36-caliber muzzleloading rifles loaded with 20 to 25 grains of FFFg or Pyrodex "P" will normally produce a muzzle velocity of around 1,500 f.p.s. with a 65-grain, .350-inch patched round ball.

Even when shooting these light loads, always attempt a head shot. A bushytail or cottontail caught dead center with a light load from a .32- or .36-caliber muzzleloading rifle can be nearly blown into two pieces.

Loaded with care, some of the smallbore muzzleloading rifles available are fully capable of producing head-shot accuracy on small game. These smallbore frontloaders do require more attention during loading than larger-bored muzzleloaders. When measuring a powder charge, take extra care to tap the side of the measure so that the charge is exactly the same for each and every shot. Even a tiny grain variation from shot to shot can mean the difference of a shot that's an inch high or low at 25 yards, which is usually the difference between a hit or a miss.

Smallbore muzzleloaders are very easily affected by fouling. After each and every shot the bore must be wiped with a damp patch to keep fouling from building in grooves that are commonly much shallower than the grooves of larger muzzleloader bores. And, when seating the patched ball over the powder charge, always use exactly the same amount of pressure on the ramrod for each load.

Muzzleloaders of .32- and .36-caliber, loaded with light powder charges and light patched round ball projectiles, produce absolutely no recoil. They are great for teaching a younger shooter the fun and challenge of muzzleloading. In the same light, there's no better way to teach the young hunter the patience of hunting with a one-shot frontloader than to take him or her after squirrels on a crisp late September or early October morning. It's great practice for experienced muzzleloading hunters, as well.

Hunting varmints can also provide some interesting off-season gunning for the black powder hunter. Not many animals normally classified as varmints will ever end up on the dinner table, so many muzzleloading hunters use the exact same rifle and load that they use for whitetails and other big game to take these often troublesome pests.

The woodchuck, popularly known as the groundhog, is a great game animal to test the shooting skills of any black powder shooter. Not many animals are as wary as the woodchuck, especially a veteran of several summers who has had close calls with long-range,

centerfire-shooting varmint hunters. Just getting within muzzleloading range can test a hunter's ability, and shots are often at 100 yards or more. There probably isn't a better way to hone a muzzleloading hunter's long-range shooting.

Prairie dogs provide the western black powder hunter with similar shooting challenges. Like the woodchuck, prairie dogs have seen considerable hunting pressure and will scurry to the safety of their den at the first sight of a hunter. Shots are normally at the outer limits of a muzzleloading rifle's effective range. Fortunately, prairie dog towns are usually on the big side, providing plenty of targets for an afternoon of shooting. Four or five hours of shooting at these little varmints will tell the shooter a lot about what he does or doesn't know about shooting his muzzleloader out past 100 yards.

Fur-bearing species such as the bobcat, fox, coyote and even the raccoon are best taken with loads that are not overly destructive. A beautiful pelt, which could fetch a good price on the fur market, is usually worthless if you blow a big hole in it. One of the smallbore muzzleloaders with a moderate 25- to 40-grain charge of FFFg black powder or Pyrodex "P" grade will deliver plenty of punch for downing a big coyote, with little damage to the fur. If you enjoy the accuracy of a larger-bored in-line rifle (below) and saboted bullets, you can also develop loads with full metal jacket handgun slugs. These do not expand and will take furbearers without much destruction.

Coyote taken with an in-line muzzleloader

Small-game hunting provides excellent opportunities to keep those muzzleloading hunting senses well tuned. In many states, some species of small game have open seasons year-round, often without any limits.

Upland Birds & Waterfowl

Hunting with black powder shotguns was all but abandoned during the first half of the twentieth century. The late 1800s saw the introduction of break-open, single-shot and double-barrel breechloading smoothbores, which were chambered for the early black powder shotshells. These developments were followed shortly by the use of modern smokeless powders and eventually the introduction of pump-action repeating shotguns and semi-autoloading shotguns.

If hunting with your lightning-fast modern pump or auto has lost some of its appeal and challenge, you may want to take a look at hunting with a slow-to-load muzzleloading shotgun. There's something about making an accurate hit with a good percussion caplock shotgun on a fast-rising pheasant, fleeing quail or running cottontail that adds greatly to the pleasures of going afield. Knowing that you may only have one good shot when hunting with a single-shot muzzleloading shotgun tends to make you concentrate on making that shot count. And even when hunting with a muzzleloading double-barrel, you are always aware of how long it takes to reload empty barrels and you're not likely to waste any shots.

The first step to hunting upland birds or waterfowl with a muzzleloading smoothbore is to select a suitable frontloader. It's unlikely that anyone will hunt regularly with a 150-year-old original. However, if you have decided to hunt with your great-great-grandfather's old muzzleloading shotgun, first have it thoroughly checked out by a competent gunsmith. The barrels on these guns are nearly always hammer-forged Damascus barrels, formed by hammering together red-hot ribbons of twisted steel around a mandrel. Through the decades, black powder fouling and corrosion could have slowly eaten away at these weak welds, making the barrels dangerous to shoot.

A good selection of side-by-side doubles and single-barreled reproductions that perform nicely on upland birds when loaded correctly are now offered by a number of companies. Most of these guns are built without any choke constriction at all. This makes it easy to stuff in proper-fitting wads, but adds to the difficulty of maintaining game-getting patterns out at any range. Experimenting with a variety of wad combinations is the only way to determine which wads perform best in an individual muzzleloading smoothbore. Traditionally, open-choked frontloading smoothbores tend to turn in their best patterns when loaded with a single .125-inch heavy over-powder card directly over the powder charge, followed by fiber or felt wads to create a 1/2- to 3/4-inch cushion between the over-powder card and shot charge. After the shot is poured in, the entire load is topped with a thin over-shot wad to keep the pellets from rolling back out the muzzle. To avoid distorting the center of the pattern, these over-shot wads are commonly made of thin cardboard of about .030-inch thickness, or a light material (cork or Styrofoam®) that easily disintegrates in front of the shot when fired.

For upland game such as pheasant, a healthy load of 90 grains of FFg black powder or Pyrodex "RS/Select" behind a 1¼-ounce load of No. 5 or 6 shot works well in most muzzleloading 12-gauge shotguns. If your target is a smaller bobwhite quail or dove, then you may find a slightly lighter 80-grain charge of FFg or "RS/Select" and 1⅛ ounces of No. 7½ or 8 shot more suitable. Whatever powder charge you settle on, always try to load a nearly equal volume of shot. This results in the best patterns from most muzzleloading scatterguns.

Today's waterfowler is faced with loading and shooting steel shot. Most duck hunters prefer No. 2 or No. 3 steel shot with a heavy powder charge of 95 to 110 grains. Goose hunters usually favor BB or No. 1 steel shot and a 100- to 110-grain powder charge. But before you load any muzzleloading smoothbore with steel shot, first check with the manufacturer to be sure that it is safe. Some of the barrels found on reproduction smoothbores may be modern steel, but could be entirely too soft for shooting steel shot. If this is the case, you could ruin a barrel with just a few rounds. Also, the barrels of most imported doubles are held together with a soft solder. Steel shot loads can cause these lead or silver solder welds to break loose.

If you plan to hunt waterfowl with a muzzleloader, you may want to concentrate on one of the modern single-barreled guns equipped with a barrel built from the same steels used in the production of modern pump or semi-auto shotgun barrels. Many of these guns feature a removable screw-in choke that can be easily replaced with a choke designed for shooting steel shot loads. One thing is certain; you'll be a lot happier with the patterns produced by one of these frontloaders – especially when presented with a 40-yard shot at a big Canada goose.

Muzzleloading Events & Organizations

Depending on who you ask, there are an estimated three to four million black powder shooters in the U.S. today. Without a doubt, most of these are hunters who turned to muzzleloading in order to cash in on the bonus hunting of the special primitive weapons big-game seasons. But for hundreds of thousands of dedicated black powder burners across the country, muzzleloading serves as something of a link to our past.

Competitions

In a few remote areas, muzzleloading never fully died out following the introduction of modern breechloading firearms and smokeless powder. Far back into the hills of Appalachia, small groups of shooters and hunters continued to use the old-fashioned frontloading guns into the 1930s. The practice eventually captured the interest of a few shooters in the Midwest, who began searching around for original muzzleloaders they could shoot in competition. In 1933, the National Muzzle Loading Rifle Association (NMLRA) was established, and modern-day muzzleloading target competition was born.

The NMLRA is still the leading organization for the muzzleloading target shooter. In addition to conducting several annual shoots (including the national muzzleloading championship at the organization's home range near the small town of Friendship, Indiana), the NMLRA also oversees competition sponsored by affiliated local and state clubs or organizations.

Most of the current NMLRA-sanctioned matches require the use of a patched round ball, and most shooting is done at paper targets at 25, 50, or 100 yards. However, muzzleloading hunters are now demanding new matches that will permit them to shoot the same rifle and load they use to hunt whitetail deer or other big game. More and more, muzzleloading clubs are conducting unlimited matches allowing the competitor to shoot a scoped frontloader that's loaded with modern saboted bullets.

Most muzzleloader matches are shot on standard paper targets of varying size, depending on the range of the match. Shooters generally have five shots for score, which is determined by how many hits arc in the 10-ring, how many are in the 9-ring, how many in the 8-ring, and so forth. (A shot is considered in a scoring ring if the center of the bullet hole lies within that ring.)

Competitors at historic encampments often shoot at small-animal targets

At the National Matches held at the NMLRA range, it may take a perfect score to walk away with top honors in some expert matches. In fact, the ⅜-inch diameter center bull of most targets is known as the "X-ring," and winners at some of the bench-rest matches have fired perfect "50-5X" scores, which means that not only were all of their hits inside the 10-ring (5 shots scoring 10 points each totals 50), but all were in the X-ring of the target (5X). In really close muzzleloading competition, the winner may be decided by some very close measurements of the bullet holes in the X-ring to determine which shooter is actually closest to dead center.

Rendezvous

For many, muzzleloading offers the opportunity to relive history. A stroll through one of the historic encampments, commonly referred to as a *rendezvous*, is like walking back into previous centuries.

Rendezvous-goers take their pursuit seriously. When fashioning their era clothing, tremendous attention is paid to every detail. The goal is to adorn attire that is authentic in every respect to the period being recreated. One of the more popular rendezvous periods represents the fur trade era of the 1830s and 1840s. The modern-day mountainman often uses the skins from game he's taken with his muzzleloader to make the buckskins he wears.

Historically accurate re-creation of the lifestyle of a certain period requires carrying a muzzleloader of the correct styling. You wouldn't want to show up at a 1770s-era Revolutionary War encampment with a circa 1840 Hawken-style percussion rifle, for example. Unless you're shooting a style of muzzleloader that would have existed during the period being relived, generally you won't be allowed to compete in any shooting competition at the encampment or rendezvous.

Rendezvous participants try to re-create the historical period in every way

You can easily spend thousands of dollars to get into this pastime. There are so many eras being re-created, it's impossible to outfit yourself satisfactorily for all of them. The French and Indian Wars, the Revolutionary War, the fur trade era and the Civil War are all being relived in full regalia today – each calls for specialized gear or clothing for the well-equipped participant. If you're consumed with interest in any of these periods, get into it slowly. Take your time to research the period clothing and equipment, and either craft or purchase items that are as authentic as possible. When it's time to participate in your first rendezvous or encampment, you'll fit in a lot better.

To seasoned rendezvousers there is nothing worse than having an ill-equipped camp set up right next door. Everyone today realizes the need for keeping food fresh in a modern insulated cooler, the necessity for personal hygiene and the modern soaps, shampoos and such needed, or getting all of your gear into camp via the ol' pickup truck or family minivan. All of these items are accepted in most camps, provided that you use the common sense to keep them out of sight. Don't ruin the historical aspect of a rendezvous by being a sloppy camper. In many camps, if you leave coolers, modern lanterns, sleeping bags and such lying around in the open, you'll be asked to leave.

Most historic camps are open to the general public, so you can visit and observe the outfits, camps and equipment required to participate. Trade blankets are usually spread out in front of just about every teepee, lean-to or tent, and are a great place to begin acquiring everything you want in order to look like and relive your favorite era.

Organizations

Muzzleloading today is a multifaceted sport. Under the umbrella of black powder shooting, you'll find a wide range of special interests. For the serious follower of each, there are a number of organizations that do an excellent job of maintaining records, promoting the sport or organizing events. Here is a look at some of the most important organizations.

NATIONAL MUZZLE LOADING RIFLE ASSOCIATION, P.O. Box 67, Friendship, Indiana 47021. Established in 1933, the NMLRA has done more to promote the sport of muzzleloading than any other organization. If you're seriously interested in shooting in muzzleloading competition, this is the organization for you (p. 121). The NMLRA's monthly publication, *Muzzle Blasts*, is filled with the dates and locations of muzzleloading shoots around the country. The results from those shoots are also published so you'll know what kind of competition you'll be facing.

American Infantry (circa 1812) reenactors in Marion, Indiana

The publication also runs technical articles on original frontloading guns from the past. You can also contact the NMLRA for the names and addresses of smaller organizations specializing in the arms and dress of just about every era of American history.

THE LONGHUNTER, P.O. Box 67, Friendship, Indiana 47021. In recognition of how the sport of muzzleloading has changed from a nostalgic interest into a true hunting sport, the NMLRA has established an organization and publication that caters entirely to the black powder hunter. The Longhunter is responsible for maintaining the records for muzzleloader-harvested big-game trophies and for publishing the *Longhunter Muzzleloading Big-Game Record Book*.

INTERNATIONAL BLACKPOWDER HUNTING ASSOCIATION, P.O. Box 1180, Glenrock, Wyoming 82637. Established in 1989, the IBHA was the first organization to cater to the wants and needs of the

dedicated muzzleloading hunter. The organization's publication, *Blackpowder Hunting*, covers muzzleloader hunting around the globe, keeping members informed about regulations, equipment changes and hunting opportunities.

NORTH-SOUTH SKIRMISH ASSOCIATION, INC., 501 N. Dixie Drive, Vandalia, Ohio 45377. Established in 1950, the N-SSA conducts a growing number of skirmish matches and Civil War era encampments around the country. Tens of thousands of authentically uniformed skirmishers gather each year to compete in the N-SSA national matches near Winchester, Virginia, creating one of the most colorful muzzleloading events currently held. If you're into shooting the big .58-caliber rifled muskets of the Civil War, you belong in this organization. Some of the most knowledgeable arms experts about the era are members of the N-SSA.

Index

Contributing Photographers (Note: T=*Top*, C=*Center*, B=*Bottom*, L=*Left*, R=*Right*, i=*inset*)

Charles J. Alsheimer
Bath, New York
©*Charles J. Alsheimer: pp. 4-5, 79T, 102-130T, 104BL, 105*

Toby Bridges
Pearl, Illinois
©*Toby Bridges: pp. 83CR, 111, 121, 122i, 120-121, 121BR*

Gary Clancy
Byron, Minnesota
©*Gary Clancy: p. 117*

Bill Kinney
BillKinney.com
©*Bill Kinney: p. 92*

Stephen W. Maas
Wyoming, Minnesota
©*Stephen W. Maas: pp. 84, 108-109*

Paramount Press, Inc.
Stow, New York
©*Robert Griffing: pp. 8-9*

James P. Rowan Photography
Chicago, Illinois
©*James P. Rowan: pp. 120-121, 123*

Rubin Photography
Eugene, Oregon
©*Ira Rubin: p. 77TR*

Leonard Rue Enterprises, Inc.
Blairstown, New Jersey
©*Irene Vandermolen: p. 6*

Contributing Muzzleloading Manufacturers:

Connecticut Valley Arms, Inc.
5988 Peachtree Corners East
Norcross, GA 30071

Dixie Gun Works, Inc.
Gunpowder Lane
P.O. Box 130
Union City, TN 38281

Knight Rifles
21852 Hwy. J46
P.O. Box 130
Centerville, IA 52544

Mountain State Muzzleloading Supplies, Inc.
#1 Muzzleloading Place
Williamstown, WV 26187

Savage Arms, Inc.
100 Springdale Road
Westfield, MA 01085

Thompson/Center Arms Co., Inc.
P.O. Box 5002
Rochester, NH 03866

Track of the Wolf, Inc.
P.O. Box 6
Osseo, MN 55369

Traditions – Performance Firearms
1375 Boston Post Road
P.O. Box 776
Old Saybrook, CT 06475